# THE FOUR RELATIONSHIPS

## Seeking Connection in a World of Disconnect

Korinn S. Hawkins

Publisher: KSH LLC

Editors: Skye Kerr Levy, Brad Wetzler, Lisa Bennett

Interior Design: Ameri Camilla

Cover Design: Ryan Lause

*Note: Some names have been changed to protect privacy.*

ISBN: 979-8-9852102-4-8

For Corey,
The hero of my heart.
Love you forever.
∞

# CONTENTS

*Whoever doesn't believe in magic and miracles,*

*doesn't have a heart open enough to see them.*

September 8, 2020

Dear Reader,

Today marks one month since the funeral of my dear, sweet husband, Corey. It has been five months since he passed away and six months since he entered the hospital with pneumonia. It has also been five and a half months since COVID-19 hit the U.S. and shut everything down, causing the delay to his funeral. It seems that during this time not only have I entered into a period of being disconnected from my life, but the whole world is also in a phase of disconnection. Maybe the circumstances that bring you to this book look different than mine, but none the less, I do not doubt that you too have familiarity with feeling disconnect. So, thank you for allowing me to show up for you today.

Back on March 9th, when Corey and I entered that emergency room *together*, we didn't know that he was fighting his biggest battle. We didn't know that he was never going to come home. We didn't know that he would have a heart attack two days before his release. When I look at today, the things I know are that it has been only 0.2 seconds since I last thought of him, since my heart looked for him to be present with me in some way, even if only in memory. It has only been one hundred and fifty-one days since I last saw his beautiful face in person, fifteen days since I last saw his face in my dreams, and zero days since I've last seen his smile and kind eyes in my mind. Twenty-two years together was not enough; I still want the lifetime.

Life is tough.

But love persists.

My life has come undone from where it used to be. I used to be a steady and solid part of a very equal team, the team of *us*: Corey and me. We were very traditional in our roles, yet there was no hierarchy—we were joined equals. We did not function separately but together. Corey worked hard for our family out of the home, and I worked hard for our family in the home. I also held a part-time job running my business as an energy therapist. Together we were strong and secure. All that strength and security feels gone.

3

Now I'm the last person standing, and all the weight that was easily distributed between two is now carried by one: me.

So, what now? What am I supposed to do with the rest of my life that was supposed to be our life? I feel like such a discombobulated mess. I keep telling God, "Okay, here I am, a blank canvas for you. Do with me what you will." (Though, I also have a few ideas of my own.) In this troubled time of unknowns and transition, I think, *Who do I really take my direction from, and how do I find my way? Where can the support be found that I feel I've lost, but still need?* I would like to ask you the same questions: where can the support that you need be found? When you feel challenged or lost, who will fill in as the other part of your team? Who can be in partnership with you in your journey? Who will help you paint that blank canvas, coloring in the lines of the rough sketch of your life?

First things first. You have to want helpers. If you have picked up this book and are curious about exploring the relationships in your life so that you can feel more connected to the life you are living, then trust that there is good company to come. Trust that there are pieces of the puzzle yet to be seen and skills yet to be learned. Very rarely does a person walk a path that no one else has walked before. Life is an individual walk, but there are others who can relate. There are other sources to take direction from in navigating the difficult unknown. When I stop to think about who is leading me in the direction that my life is going today, at first glance it seems a combination of God and myself, using that inner compass that I believe we all have. But with a closer look, I see that I also take direction from the people in my life. People are relational and so others do affect us. Our loved ones, mentors, neighbors, friends, and children help form and guide our decisions every day. We also get direction from the world at large from the way of the world and the way of the earth. For instance, if it is cold outside, you wear warmer clothes. Or, in relation to the time I am writing this: if you are in a pandemic, you wear a mask.

The direction that you are being given in life is relational, complex, and multifaceted. As much as humans might want to compartmentalize and give one area credit for who they are or how they are, there are really no lines that separate the areas. Who you are and how you are is a product of so many things: nature and nurture, past events and future hopes, effort and luck, mood and mind, others and self, God and earth, location and role, drive and rest, culture and society, belief and disbelief, science and art. You are not easily definable by a single facet of your life because you are, in all your wholeness, beautifully undefinable. It's the urge to define that puts you in a box and gives you confining labels: I am this or I am not that. However, it is the will to create that lets you grow beyond them.

One can say I am who I am because of God, because of my personal efforts, because of the people in my life, or because of the circumstances I was born into or subjected to. A person can compartmentalize with any one of these statements, but that is not the full truth because even though you can procure a sense of direction based off any *one* of these influences, they *all* converge into relationship. Relationship, as connection, is the binding force. Relationship permeates all of these areas. And relationship is something that, as a willful and creative being, you must navigate.

One thing I noticed after the loss of my husband was that even though it felt like my life had stopped, everyone else's lives kept moving forward. In forward movement, others suffered loss and challenge too. Some had financial, physical, or mental health issues come up. Some had hardship at work or in home life. All while life kept moving forward each day. In my pain, I could see even more clearly that *no one* is immune to pain. No one is immune to adversity. It is as if we all are in boats that have to maneuver rough seas, no matter if our boats come in different sizes, shapes, and colors. Having hardship is human. How you respond to it is what makes it bearable or unbearable. In my own life, I have seen an underlying truth that connection soothes hardship while disconnect deepens its burden. Could it be that we are all the same in this regard: separation hurts; connection soothes? I will ask you: is disconnection intensifying your hardship? Might connection soothe it?

This book will lead you through an inner and outer journey along the pathway of relationship. It is written to help you gain understanding and take action. It takes you through each of the four relationships: with God, self, others, and earth. And it leads you to the relational root: the heart. It is these four relationships together that make up the fullness of living. If you lack in having connection in one of these relationships, the lack reaches out across the others. This is why gaps that are missing need filling, because you cannot be complete without having connection to that which completes you. What you will discover through this book is that the inner and outer journey, though two seemingly different directions, are really one thing: a pathway to openness.

The first two chapters invite you into a space of looking with new eyes to see the dimensionality of connection so that you can experience it in a deeper way. From there you will dive into four consecutive chapters, each one focusing on one of the four relationships: self, others, God, and earth. The last two chapters focus on bringing it all together, and giving you a plan to move forward. I will share my life with you along the way but my bigger aim is to support you in connecting to your own life.

There are two ways to get in to touch with yourself that are the foundation of this book: experience and knowledge. Being self-aware in your *experience* of yourself educates you, and gaining *knowledge* educates you, too. Both give perspective and tools to use for living and growing. The self-experience sections in this book are called *Awareness Exercises* and the self-knowledge sections are called *Time for Insight*. I highly recommend that you get a journal or notebook to write your reflections in. This may be especially helpful to look back at when you approach the end of the book and the torch is passed to you to spread a light of openness in your life. The torch you will carry forward comes in the form of a strategic plan that you will create in the final chapter. This vision will give you a game plan for building relationship and soothing your life and its challenges through increased heart connection.

As I sit in my sunroom writing this letter of today, addressed to the you of tomorrow, I glance down and notice that my cup of tea has a little tag with a bit of wisdom offered. I hold it between my fingers and read what it says. I smile to myself, feeling a pregnant pause of so much more going on under the surface of me jumping into this project. This is how the world speaks to me, this is how my life speaks to me—in little winks, nudges, and inner feelings calling me to pay attention. So much is held in just a moment. I can feel it.

Every facet of connection can be so beautifully woven into the big events of our lives but also into the mundane ones. Mundane like reading this tea bag, which says, "Give happiness and you will end up happy." How simple and yet how deeply true. Give happy to get happy sounds so deliciously uncomplicated. As human beings sometimes it is easy to forget the value of simplicity, and the purity in it. People are beautifully and purposefully complex, yet our complexity can confuse and complicate. Perhaps instead of being so complex it would be helpful to be a little bit simpler in your direction in life, like this tea bag quote. Get back to basics. Get back to the center. To the core. To the heart.

The heart is all about connection. And connection is the vehicle for relationship, as you must connect to relate. The joy of relationship is also connection. Connection is both the means and the medicine. Synonymous to what the tea bag wisdom is saying: be giving and the giving will give to you. Be giving to God. Be giving to yourself. Be giving to others. And for heaven's sake, be giving to the earth.

Now, I invite you to give yourself time and give each of these four relationships attention and openness and see what is given to you in return.


With a sincere heart,


Korinn

# 1

# CONNECTION

## The Medicine of Relationship

I was a wounded, sad-eyed, sixteen-year-old leaving a New Year's Eve party to sit alone in my car and wait. Wait for the flannel-wearing seventeen-year-old boy more interested in the loud excitement of the party than in leaving with me. I was tired and ready to go home. He could not pull himself away. The draw of the party scene was too intoxicating. I had been sitting on the couch in the living room quietly watching people in the kitchen. Having told him several times that I was ready to go, he knew I was waiting on him. And yet there I sat, feeling the letdown of not being enough to compete with a good party. Finally, I got up and walked over to him, leaned down to his ear, and said, "I'm going out to the car. If you want a ride, you need to come out now." And I left. I didn't even give him a chance to reply. I was his ride, so he had to come out, right? I was taking a bold step in trying to push him to make the decision that I wanted him to make. Now or never. Let's go.

We had been yo-yoing, breaking up and then getting back to together, for months, and the strings of attachment were wearing thin. We were in this strange place of letting go and holding on. Holding onto the time put in over the last year and a half where our lives had become intertwined. We went to school together during the day and when I wasn't working after school, I was usually at his house or driving around with him to hang with friends. Holding onto the love and at the same time letting go of the love is such a complicated place to be. But in moving closer towards letting go, I was letting go of the dysfunction, the hurt feelings, the immature manipulation, and the hope of things getting better.

Sitting alone in my car, letting the engine warm up in the wintery night, I was feeling that I had a different place I should be. He had not followed me when I left the kitchen, so I sat a while longer in the driveway, thinking maybe that would change. I listened to the radio as I watched the snow softly come down and melt into droplets on the windshield, and then something mystically fortuitous happened. The radio channel changed by itself and settled into "Soul to Squeeze" by the Red Hot Chili Peppers. I whipped my head to the right to look straight-on at the radio. Sitting there staring in shock, my attention was grabbed, and I listened intently.

"Where I go, I just don't know

I got to, got to, gotta take it slow

When I find my peace of mind

I'm gonna give ya some of my good time."

I felt a sadness release in my heart as I dropped my head and closed my eyes. The song was singing my life to me. I felt myself sitting at a crossroads of the unknown, making the choice to leave behind a person, a way of being, a repeating pattern that was no longer working for me. I was unsure of myself but lifted up by the idea that when I get to where I am going, things would be better. Clarity was ringing like a bell in my mind telling me: "It is time to do something different with your life."

What I chose to do in that next moment was to put my car into reverse, back out from where I was, and move in a different direction: away from the night and away from the way in which I had been in relationship with the other person and with myself. I not only felt—I knew—it had been the hand of God that reached through, changing the frequency of the radio, as if to say, "Listen here, little one. I have something for you to hear and something for your heart to feel. An ending and a beginning." I took myself back home that night. Not only to where I lived, but to where I needed to be: home within myself. Coming into alignment with my inner, wiser self, as I re-centered my priorities and put myself first.

As I think back to that time, I am in awe of the sudden sense I had of how to steer my own ship. And I am grateful for the inner call to do so. Into uncharted territory I went, with a sad but hopeful heart. Choosing me over we, I was able to maneuver out from under a thumb that had been holding me down. I began to place more value on who I was and became stronger in doing so. I felt a strength to withstand any coercion to turn in another person's direction that was not my own. With more self-connection, more connection with God, better standards for human relationship, and an openness to see what the world might bring, I held the authority to change course and set the stage for what was to come in my life.

During this time, I was ready to shift out of an immature relationship; to not be held by it but to instead grow *because of it*. Starting at a place of not knowing "where I go," but hearing "peace of mind" as the theme song calling out to me, I moved forward in life. This lyric resonated as life began to dance through me in a stronger way.

Do you ever hear that little whisper telling your heart you need a change? No matter where you are in life, you are never without the potential to steer in a different direction. And finding the direction you want to be steering towards takes awareness, honesty, heart—and sometimes it takes letting go. Can you hear the song: "Where I go, I just don't know. I got to, got to, gotta take it slow"? Can you feel life dancing through you? Saying that when you get to where you are going, you will have goodness to share from where you came.

## Defining Relationship

As a young girl experiencing my relationship with everything that night, I was opened to feel—to feel the earth and its quiet snowy scene wrapping around me as I heard the nudge of God and the calling from within myself to be in new relationship with others.

*Relationship* is defined as the condition of being connected. There is much we are connected to in life, and the condition of our connections vary. Connections can be distant or close, suffocating or liberating, orienting or cause disarray. One thing that can be said about all relationships is that they are ever-evolving—sometimes they are catalysts propelling us forward, sometimes stagnant vices holding us back. Sometimes relationships feel secure and cozy in ways you never want to part with. But they are always a source for growth and awareness if you are open to learning.

Through your life experiences of beginnings and endings, and ups and downs, you can arrive in a place of realizing that there is much to learn and that goodness and growth can come out of change and challenge. Relationships are the framework through which you grow and move through life. Relationships are never one-sided though, so let us now look at the structure and nature of relationship. To form a relationship, there are always at least two things relating to each other. And just as life is not meant to be a cakewalk, by design, relationships are not always easy. They can sometimes feel like a tangled mess. You may have played a part in the tangling, even if passively. Yet, you can always take a hand to the untangling, too. To do this, it helps to step back and have a wider view.

## Awareness Exercise

We don't usually think about it this way, but you are literally in relationship with everything that surrounds you right now—including where you are sitting. This exercise is an opportunity to explore this connection.

- ○ First, feel your feet, legs, bottom, and back all in position against where you sit. You are in relationship with the earth—the physical matter that is the chair or the place in which you sit.

o   Now think about how it is that you came to be sitting here in this place. How did things align so that you could carve out some time to sit and read a book—here, now, just for you? You are in relationship with yourself.

o   How did this book come to be in your hands in this moment and this place? You are in relationship with others.

o   Even further back, how did you *really* come to be so that you could be here, as you, in this chair on the earth today? You are in relationship with God.

And all of this is wrapped up into one simple moment. Your life is incredible.

## Changing How to Look at Relationship

I have been able to have moments through the course of my life where I could step back and see a bigger view. Moments where I think deeper, stranger even. Sometimes it is something simple that then catches me and causes my mind to float away, volleying between wonder and logic. One warm fall day for example, I was sitting at the old maple table in our sunroom, the perfect spot for school work and writing. As I was working on one section of a chapter in this book, my eyes kept glancing up and out of the windows that line the front of our house. Noticing the day was waning as the sky was starting to shade itself in pinks, yellows, and oranges. Randomly, a thought came to me about how the sunset is never-ending. And with that simple thought, down the rabbit hole I went, contemplating how the sunset keeps wrapping itself around the world in a continuous band of gorgeous color. My mind led on, taking me a bit further into thinking about how this happens over and over, day after day.

In this quiet moment of pausing from the task at hand and being with my thoughts, another notion layered in as my awareness expanded to realizing that it is always sunset *and* sunrise somewhere in the world. I thought about how it is really *two* bands of light coloring and circling our world, over and over. They are chasing each other but never meeting. Or, wait . . . maybe they meet where the two sides become one? I wonder if they meet at the top and the bottom of the earth and connect there? I wonder if the sunrise and the sunset are really one thing? I think further still, picturing an unbreakable chain of light that just holds steady, as it is actually the earth that is moving.

My thoughts were getting away with me in a beautiful sort of way. Allowing time for reason and wonder to meander together in curiosity about the way things are. This is how my mind works sometimes, which I feel helps expand the scope of my view. Having these contemplative thought-chains can open our eyes to seeing the relationship between things a little differently. In this case, the connectedness of the sunrise and the sunset, and its continuous steady beauty.

Having this built-in curiosity and the ability to take a step back allows us to look at things that are more complex, less definitive. Things that aren't as easily provable through Google research: like the meaning of death or what really happens when we die. There are times now when I sit on the front porch in my rocking chair, next to Corey's that now sits empty, and I think of him and his death. On days like this, as I watch the sunset softly sweep in, its gorgeous colors soothe and hush the day and my soul. I think about some of the last words I said to him. In the hospital, as I held him for the last time, in the moments before his soul was ready to lift from this life, I put my lips against his ear and whispered, "We'll be together again, baby. When I die, let's meet on the beach at sunset." I have played this meeting over and over in my mind so many times. I can see him there, standing in the ignited light of the sky against the water and the sand. There are two wooden beach chairs there for us to sit in and catch-up, like we used to do here on our front porch, with the sunset shining down on us.

In those moments when I sit and watch the light of day come to an end, empty chair beside me, I wonder if there is a reflection of the workings of death echoed out in the light of the sunset. I look out at the color and can almost feel it as the light of heaven's love radiating through. As the pink shines through at the base of the horizon, I smile to myself and call it, "The rose of the sky." I take it in through my captivated eyes and let it land on my heart as God offering a symbol of his love in its soft pink. Perhaps this band of color and light, in its celestial origin, is not only a part of what brings day and night but a part of what brings death and life. The sunset as one steady band and God as one steady hand, passing over our world, as the world moves, as life moves in continual beginnings and endings. I am now brought back around to an awareness that I have come to see: an awareness that there is relationship in everything. And how relatedness can be seen when one steps back to a bigger view.

In a more internal sense, when you look at relationship being everywhere and with everything, you can come to see that you are a center point for it all. You are at the center of every relationship that you have because you are *where* you experience all of it from. You are the body and soul that has the eyes to see, the ears to hear, and the heart to feel all of the intricacies that are your unique experience of life from your unique vantage point. And did you know that when you get up, you just might leave an imprint on where you've been? This too is relationship. Relationship, as I mentioned above, is the state of being connected. And you are connected to a whole heck of a lot you think about and a whole heck of a lot you don't. Chances are you weren't thinking about your chair or how it felt against your body until the exercise brought the topic up. And what about the places in your life that you are connected to but never think of? Or those places in your life that you feel disconnected from but that you are actually still connected to? Bringing awareness to disconnect is important for seeing clearer so that you can actually become more connected to your life.

## The Danger in Disconnect

There is a real danger in regards to disconnect because being unaware is a danger. Imagine it like this: every day when you come home, you're carrying a big, heavy bag. Let's call it baggage. Only let's say you don't pay attention to how your baggage affects your surroundings. When you walk through your door, you have the habit of tossing your big, heavy bag into a basket on the floor. You never look to see how it lands so, you don't notice the damage being done over time: it makes dings and scratches on the wall; the edge of the basket where it lands is starting to become misshapen; and the innocent bystander of a potted ficus tree has one section with no leaves left because it keeps getting knocked into. You don't notice any of this because you are in your unconscious pattern of throwing your bag to put it away.

I'm talking figuratively here about things being damaged by throwing your baggage around, but what about when we start talking about people and the effect that unconscious habits or behaviors have? That is when the real damage can be done. What about if we are in unconscious relationship to God and the earth? What damage is happening? Most times, if you pause in your patterning and look closer, you will see where things need to change. You'll see you are dinging up your wall, smashing your basket, and disrupting your trees growth. And you'll realize that that is not actually what you want. Yes, sometimes we are innocent in our unconsciousness, yet still it is a danger because its effect is real.

There is disconnect in the world today in general. People are being groomed to be in opposition to others. There is a whole industry developed around how human beings are impressionable—it's called marketing and advertisement—but it also includes propaganda and censorship. It seems the use of human impressionability has taken a nasty turn into making people the commodity. Human attention is being harvested to take a side. Driven like cattle, people are losing touch with the fact that we all are human beings. Polarization can be unconscious and unintentional, but sometimes it is deliberate with the aim of a conscious manipulation. We see polarization in such places as media, social media, and politics, in race, religion, and cultural opinion, and even in medical and health opinions.

This extreme polarization is dangerous because it disconnects large groups of people from being open to see that one view is not the only view. It also keeps people from admitting that maybe the view they hold is not without fault. One place I see this is when I turn on the news, where I am aware that there is a consistent pattern of pointing fingers and deflecting blame. Where can the connections be made that are needed to come together for the sake of peace? Sadly, it appears all of this has been fueling division and closed minds, instead of helping people know that they can still be on the same team, even when they have differences. But your focus here is just you. Phew, right? Yet I think that cultivating greater connection in your life inevitably creates a beautiful ripple effect.

I also believe it is true that sometimes even when we *do* look at things, they aren't so clear. After all, we don't know what we don't see. If we are not conscious of what we are missing, then there is no inkling to look. There is fundamental detachment. It could be as obvious as the morning alarm going off to wake you up, but you are too sound asleep, trailed off in the la-la land of a dream, that isn't the reality you are living in. There is a cost to living this way: detached, unaware, walking through life asleep, or hiding from people, opportunity, connection, or relationship.

The cost is that you are not living a full life; you are living a portion of a life. You are not living to your full potential and not making the impact that you are capable of: for others, the world, and God's plan. This detachment can affect you physically by making your energy heavy and sluggish, which translates to your physical vitality being degraded. It can affect you spiritually in that the light source of inspiration seems to miss you, and you lack a luster for life. It can affect you mentally by adding to social anxiety, worthiness issues, and depression. And it can affect you emotionally by closing down your natural human feelings, which are purposeful and serve a function for your wellness.

The flip side of this detachment is engagement. It is in the bravery to face yourself. Having the courage to look into those spaces of life that are hard to give attention to because you don't feel connected to them. In connecting, you will gain strength, understanding, and even more connection. In giving attention to anything that you are in relationship with, the relationship is allowed the space to develop. When you grow things with openness, care, and compassion, they become fruitful and beautiful.

## Unawareness is Disconnect

Sitting at home one day, I got wrapped up in getting a chunk of writing done. I had been at it all afternoon, only taking breaks to go to the bathroom or refill my iced tea. Sitting in the brightly lit sunroom at the front of the house, I saw the kids' bus pull up. Next, I saw my son, Gavin, walking up the driveway. I tried to peek around the blind spot of the window to see my daughter. I couldn't see her but thought: *She must have gotten off. She's probably just walking in the yard somewhere.*

When Gavin came through the front door, I asked: "Where's Marin?"

"Where's Marin!?" he said.

That's when it hit me. *Oh no, I was supposed to pick her up from school.* I had been so engrossed in my work that the time slipped away. It was 4:00 and I was supposed to have picked her up at 3:15. As I grabbed my keys, threw on my shoes, and fumbled with my phone to try to call the school, I felt frazzled, scared, saddened, and embarrassed. I had been taken over by living unconsciously. One-track minded, I didn't even notice the clock or think to check it.

By the time I got to the school, I was in tears, so sorry that I had done that to her. As soon as I got to her in the office, I hugged her and told her, "I am so sorry."

She told me, "It's okay, Mom. Everyone makes mistakes."

Her forgiveness and compassion were medicine to us both. Your forgiveness and compassion for yourself in hard areas of disconnect can also be medicine. This is why the healthier your connections are, the more cohesive you feel in your life. The connection smooths over your rough edges and heals you. Being unconscious in making mistakes is what it is—something to work on. Being conscious in apologizing or conscious in forgiving is its powerful opposite.

## Consciousness is Connection

The perception of detachment or disconnection is not the ultimate truth. The ultimate truth is that you are still connected to that which you feel disconnected from. I was disconnected from remembering to pick-up my daughter, but that didn't change that she was still there to pick-up. We sometimes forget to give attention to our emotions or life circumstances, but that does not make them go away. But let's take a step back for a moment and simplify things. Think back to the awareness exercise you did of noticing the place you are sitting. Now think about two minutes before that: were you consciously aware of how your body was resting against the space you take, or were you in your mind, thinking about other things? Me too. But did the fact that you were not consciously aware of how your body felt against the seat make the connection any less real? Did it make the underlying, subtle relationship of your body to the chair any different? No, it did not. This is a glimmer of something bigger. How your quality of conscious relationship is what makes up your life. Again, bringing *you* to be the central core of all of your relationships. Your awareness or conscious vantage point comes from only one set of eyes: yours. And with the right eyes to see how the connections in your life are important to your very being, you can feel depth, richness, and support through your actively lived experience of connecting.

There are four connected areas that make up the total of all relationships you could ever have in life. I will be using the four-leafed clover as a symbol to express this. Think of yourself as being the four-leafed clover; each leaf is an aspect of relationship. The four relationships are: with God, with yourself, with other people, and with the earth. Each of the four relationships are a dedicated area all their own, but they are also each connected at the center of things. In their connection they together make up the whole of who you are. But more than that, these four relationships together are your lucky four-leafed clover; with them all, you have something special that is meant to bring goodness into your life.

## Time for Insight

Take some time now to get a personal gauge of your current connectedness by opening up your journal and jotting down your thoughts.

- List who *and* what are the things in your life. Your relationships are more than just with people, so be sure to list both by making a column for *who* (people) and a column for *what* (factors).

- Ask yourself: *do I feel close or distant from each of these connections?* Write a plus mark by each that you feel close to and a minus mark by each that you feel distant from.

- For those where you put a minus mark, ask yourself: *do I feel disconnected to the point of feeling like there is no connection there at all?* If so, put a circle with a line through these ones, to express a feeling of no connection.

- Now look at the ones that you marked as feeling close to and ask: *does this give me a sense of wholeness?* Circle these ones.

Each circle is symbolic of connection. The open circles show there is openness in your connection. The circles that have a slash through them show that you are closed in your connection. What you are looking at, what is staring back at you from this page in your journal, is how relationships impact your life as the framework you grow in. Some of the connections here are open for growth, others are closed off from allowing growth. In general, a person either grows towards wholeness in connection or is fragmented in disconnection. Connection has the ability to join together pieces, while disconnect severs pieces from the whole. I applaud you for taking the time to get in touch with where you are starting at in your relationships.

## Diversity in Relationships

Each relationship is different, yet all have a purpose in your life. How can you expect positive change in how you relate inside yourself and outside, if you do not open up a dialogue of conscious awareness to hear what connections are prompting you to grow, which are falling stagnant in latency, and which are simply treasures of heartwarming comfort to hold? Each relationship has purpose to grasp.

Relationships are as diverse as the trillions of cells in your body. In fact, let's take the body as an example: at a glance, each cell has the same general biological composition. These include cell membrane, a nucleus, and cytoplasm. But in function, each is carrying out miraculously diverse and purposeful acts of life, such as cells for breath, for heartbeat, and for mind and feeling. Each cell is individual yet functions as part of a whole. Could it be that we cannot function as a whole without coming together in our individual functions? Could it be there is purpose in our individuation, in our widespread locations, and specializations? How could there not be when this is the design of life down to the cellular level. Differences together.

Relationships are as multifaceted as the specialized cells in your body. Some enable you a breath of fresh air, some get circulation or movement pumping through your being, and some cause a sharp pain if a nerve is set-off and inflamed. The breath of fresh air could be related to a moment you finally get to yourself to sit down and enjoy something just for you. The movement pumping could be the earth's global social unrest that is crossing over into your life and motivating you to act for a larger purpose. The sharpness could be that person in your life who causes you a little twinge of *oh no* when you see them, triggering a response of closing off.

## Duality in Relationship

To simplify the complexity of relationships, we are going to look at them as dualistic, or two-sided, in one specific dimension: connection. Picture one coin: it has two sides, but the coin is still just one thing. The coin is relationship and the two sides are connection and disconnection, as they are opposite states of connectedness. But both sides are relationship. The relationship you have with any given thing is either one supportive of connection or of disconnection.

The example of getting time for yourself as a breath of fresh air—that is connecting. You are fostering a chance to connect with something that gives you joy. In the example of the earth's social unrest getting your blood pumping to take action—that could play as two different qualities of flame to the same fire, depending on your level of openness. It could play to the quality of flame being illuminating light, supportive in connecting you to like-minded individuals who stand for the same ideal. But it could also play to the destructive quality of the burn of the flame in being supportive to disconnection as you enter into the polarizing or warring mindset of us *vs.* them. And in the example of feeling a sharp twinge when someone bothersome to you appears, you close off from being open to the moment because you contract against the discomfort you have previously felt near them. This disconnect does what disconnect does: divides you and keeps you from feeling whole, or from seeing that someone else is.

## The Truth of Unity in Duality

When it is forgotten that one is *always* in connection, you see the world with more duality than unity. Unity is that sense that everything is connected. When most people think of duality, they think of everything being in opposition but that's not entirely true. Do you know that we have a perfect symbol that expresses duality held within oneness? It is the yin-yang symbol from ancient China known in Eastern Taoism.

When I was a teenager, sitting in class in high school, uninterested in what was being taught, I would half-listen and half-focus on scribbling designs on notebook paper with my pen. I used to doodle things like peace signs and yin-yang symbols. I would draw the circle and then separate it with the curvy line through the middle. Then I would make two little circles in each half, being careful to only shade in one of the circles and one of the halves on opposite sides. This symbol was familiar to me, but I had no real concept of what I was drawing. That knowledge came later in life when I started down the path of learning about energy. Then what I learned was that this symbol is a directional view of how *oneness is separated into duality*. It illustrates how all is one and that everything in the one has a purposeful balance of opposites existing within it.

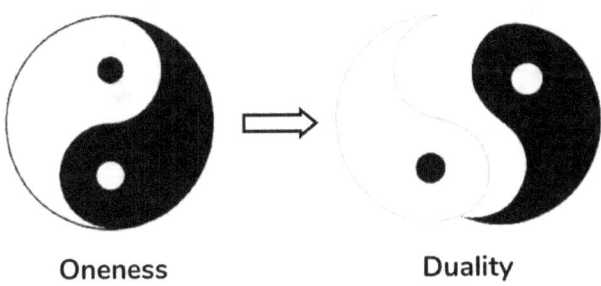

**Oneness**     **Duality**

There is a complimentary Western concept that is a directional view of *bringing duality into oneness*. It is in Christianity, in bringing the dualistic human heart, capable of good and evil, to oneness in loving God. In the Christian model this also brings a person into oneness by being a member of the body of Christ (God) on earth. Interestingly, there are also two components that make up this symbol. This parallel was made evident when the two broken-down components of the cross were shared with me by Kevin Niv Farrow as I was training with him to become a Spirit Level AcuEnergetics® Meditation Instructor. He talked about the ancient practice of the Mystic Cross meditation that works to open up the energy centers of the light body. He taught how the symbol of the cross is the *unio mystica*—the mystical union of man and the divine. The horizontal line is symbolic of our earth connection and the vertical line is symbolic of our heaven connection. The two opposites combine to make the Christian symbol of unity: the cross.

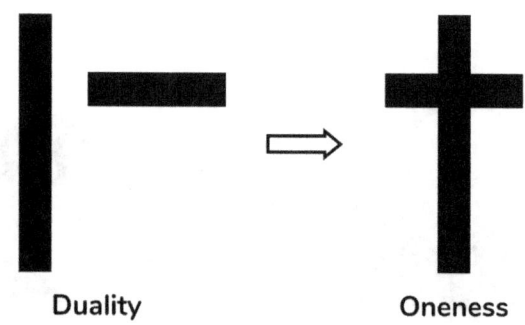

**Duality**                    **Oneness**

In their simplicity, the cross and the yin-yang symbol each echo the same thing: the existence of duality and unity. Yet in their complexity, they are in seeming opposition as constructs of thought to follow and live by. The One is the two; the two are the One[1]. However, both are each a side on the same coin, and that coin is the spiritual experience of being human. The experience that oneness is separated in us in our duality but that actually at the same time our duality is what brings us back into wholeness or oneness. The sameness connecting us is that we are *all* spirits being human. We all have human duality and we all have spiritual oneness. There is the One, there is the source to life, and all are a part of this life source. So, it can be said that you are both the same as the source and different from it. Is rain any different than a river? They both are water. One is the source and one is the location. Duality in oneness. Wholeness in duality.

Take another look at the yin-yang symbol as duality in wholeness. There is the yin side, which is black with a white dot, and the yang side is white with

---

[1] One is capitalized as to refer to God in His oneness

a black dot. The reason there is a little bit of the other in each of them is because there is no separation—the two sides exist together. They are not mutually exclusive; they are dependent on the other for movement, for motion. Perhaps even for existence. Night chases day, awake follows asleep. What goes up, must come down. Boy meets girl. The sperm and the egg. The yin and the yang *are* what makes the world go round. Negative things can inspire positive actions; and sometimes positive things can be crushed by a negative.

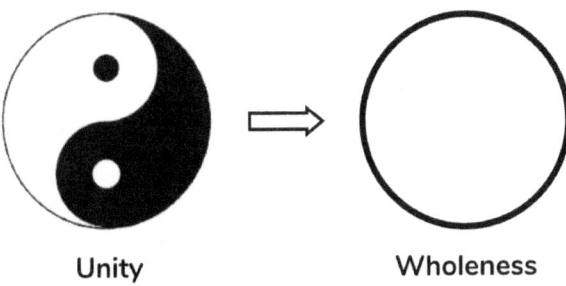

**Unity**          **Wholeness**

Now, bring your attention to the wholeness. The two sides together make up the whole. It is the good *and* the bad, the day and the night, your pain and your love that are whole together. Heaven and earth are really not so far apart because in true essence they are One. Heaven and earth are One in God, and God is the One. In general yin is regarded to be female, passive, earth energy and yang as male, active, heaven energy. Every person has both yin and yang within them as passive and active energy. To put it simply, every person has both dimensions of passive *being* and active *doing* in them. We are all by nature God's *do-ers* and his *be-ers*. God's yin and God's yang is His[2] oneness within us but also is His oneness across humanity as a whole because human beings are

---

2 The pronoun His in referring to God is not meant to imply gender. It is just what is most familiar for me to use when speaking of God.

His girls and His boys that create the motion to make the world go round and that make it grow in number, and in depth.

## Duality's Double Vision

Do you believe we are all connected? It sometimes seems like that part of being human is lost. Do you believe what affects one can affect many? We all live on the same one earth, are nourished the same through food and water, and breathe from the same pocket of air contained within our planet. All people can walk in the same way, upright, on two feet. We use the same muscles in our mouths and throats to talk, use the same capacity of the heart to love. Yet we are so separated, so divided, by things we *see* as separate. These things include physical or geographical distance and mental or emotional distance as well. Yet, it is possible for people to circle back to being united in that which makes them different: united in *being* human despite human difference.

There are two potential views to see here so it is like having double vision. One perspective tends to dominate how you view the world—so, do you see with unity on the connection side of the coin or with separation on the disconnected side of the coin? Both are there to see.

I will use my current situation as an example. As a widow, I am aware that I am now different, with a different view in mind. I am a single mom in a sea of married couples with families. Viewing this through connection and feeling unity, I can see things with the perspective: "This has been so painful, *but* I feel like what has helped me can be good for others feeling the same way. I want to share what I know and learn from others too."

The flip side, viewing my world through disconnect and feeling separateness, may have the perspective: "This has been so painful, and I feel like nothing is going to change. I might as well just get used to being unhappy. There is no help for me."

Feeling alone and hopeless is something that people feel. But is it how you feel from time to time, or is it how you feel all of the time? Do you keep flipping your coin to the side of connection—seeking where there are others like you who you can learn from and give to? Or, are you keeping your coin on the side of disconnect—focusing on how dramatically different your life is from those around you and feeling buried in it?

## Sameness in Emotion

About a month after Corey's death, my friend Pearl lost both her son and her ex-husband in a tragic accident. At the time, I was sunk in my own emotional deep end and was not able to be there for her much. I needed all my energy to be there for my children and for myself. Yet my heart understood; she too had been blind-sided and was swept into the downward spiral of loss. Pearl was good about continuing to reach out, we shared some grief resources, and loosely kept in touch despite being individually consumed in the fog of grief. During one such check-in, Pearl shared that she had two other friends who also had suffered recent losses of spouse, mother, and father. In her generous spirit's wisdom, she saw how we each might benefit from connecting with each other and felt called to bring us purposefully together for support. She organized a Zoom chat, to which I showed up wounded and sad, but open. It ended up that Pearl and the two women I was meeting for the first time gave the perfect space for the relatable connection my soul was craving: someone to understand. As we each took turns sharing and crying, I noticed the effortlessness of being able to both breathe in another's experience of grief and to breathe out my own. Each of our losses were unique, yet we were *all* in the tumbling throes of the aftermath and easily connected because of our sameness in feeling raw pain. In that first call, I was made to feel that the grief, though individual, was shared. In that there was comfort.

Because you are a part of the collective of human beings on this one, wide-open earth, you have similarity with others in your feelings. Even the feeling of loneliness is shareable. However, while it is very true that you are in your unique experience of whatever you are going through in your life right now, it is also true that there is someone out there who can relate. There is a commonality in what you are feeling. That can be a connection point. People who are lonely understand loneliness in others. People who are survivors understand the stamina or drive in other survivors. People who are grateful can see what others have to be grateful for. What one can see in themselves opens doors to understanding and connecting with others.

People may feel connected or disconnected due to differing things but the way in which people feel them is a program in our humanness that stretches beyond our individualism. It is a collective feeling. If someone says something makes them happy or sad, you understand it because you know from your unique experience what happy and sad feel like. The colors of emotion are all there. The depth of the colors might be different, yet still recognizable in others. Sad is sad. Happy is happy. This is experienced for example, in the phenomena of watching movies that make you cry or make you laugh; you feel that universal emotion that courses through us all. Different things make people cry or laugh yet all have known crying and laughing. Or just like if anyone gets a nail driven through their foot, they feel pain, you share in global feelings because you share in humanness. There is only one humanity, and you, your neighbor, and the foreigner across the world are all a part of it.

## Shared Humanness in Connection

When you feel connected, you feel included. You feel part of something. You feel valued, acknowledged, and inspired in goodness. When you feel disconnected, you feel separate, left out, unworthy, undervalued, unacknowledged—more saddened and angry than inspired for good. Disconnect shows up multidimensionally across social, global, and personal issues. It shows up across people, culture and land, worship, and belief. Every place where disconnect shows up, separation persists and chokes out unity. But unity is never not there; in disconnect you just don't see it because *it is the coin in its wholeness.* You are looking at the two sides and only seeing that either it's heads or it's tails and missing the wholeness of both sides being there to see. Unity is there, quietly standing in the fullness of what has already been created: you, and them, on God's green earth, and by the Creator himself. Disconnection is a problem and leads to problems, but it is only ever just a fragmented version of the oneness that innately is. Similar to how people share in feeling their emotions; we all share in feeling a natural pull towards having human connection.

## The Difference between Connection and Disconnect

Disconnection → leads to dissolution which → leads to separateness,

where the viewpoint is as an outsider. Two sides.

Connection → leads to integration which → leads to unity,

where the viewpoint is as an insider. One whole.

Through connection, we are in a state of greater integration and can feel more whole or in alignment with oneness despite duality existing. In contrast, through disconnection, we are in a state of greater dissolution and feel more fragmented. This creates a skewed view to give more attention to duality *vs.* oneness. Duality is what then cyclically keeps us feeling separate. It's like being in that rut again of feeling stuck in being alone. The feeling of being on our own hardens the heart against letting others in to share life's challenges with. The cycle of feeling alone is perpetuated by actions that reinforce that you stay in that state, not actively seeking connection as your solution.

What does it mean to be disconnected? You are at odds with the thing you feel disconnected from. As a human being, you can feel disconnected with yourself or a part of yourself, with others, with a role you have, or with a part of your life. For example, you can disconnect from your body in feeling that you don't have the ideal height, shape, size, attractiveness, or physical ability. These aren't things that matter in the big picture of self-worth, but maybe in your disconnect to being whole, you think that they do and so in the space between being what you are and what you are not, a disconnect is established. And in that disconnect, it is hard to accept yourself in your wholeness because you feel at odds with yourself.

What does it mean to be connected? You are in alignment with the thing you feel connected with. Again, feeling connected can be cross-categorical.

You can feel connected to yourself, others, God, and the earth. To give the flip-side of the above example: someone who feels connected to their body has an integrated (not dissolving) relationship with himself or herself. This adds to them feeling whole rather than fragmented. Someone who is connected to their body might still see themselves as not having the ideal height, shape, size, attractiveness, or physical ability but that one little self-opinion does not leverage against their self-worth and self-value. They have a bigger awareness of who they are as a being because they have not separated their wholeness into categories of perfect and imperfect attributes. They are connected into being who they are, letting the things that shine about them shine. They tolerate, with love and acceptance, the *oh wells*. *Oh well, I've got dimples, wrinkles, and crinkles in all the wrong places; my body is my friend because I cannot go anywhere without it, so I value taking care of it, and it taking care of me.*

Disconnection is a toxic troublemaker and connection is a healing unifier. In the state of the world, one can see many examples of the destructive dissolution that comes through feeling separate in disconnection. But the world is just as equally a humbling place to see the integration that comes through connection. And beyond a global perspective, I think all people individually can look at their own personal lives and identify areas where disconnection and connection can be seen. Take a moment here to explore this for yourself and write down your insight in your journal.

## Time for Insight

- Globally, where do you see disconnect?
- Globally, where do you see connection?
- Where personally do you feel disconnect in your life?
- Where personally do you feel connection in your life?

Both are here, connection and disconnection. They exist together as the Eastern and Western concepts also exist together. Perspective is either unifying or separating, but the potential to see both is there. Hopefully each difference is purposefully playing off the other to propel you towards reaching for the unknown where you'll find peace of mind and have goodness to offer. There are moments that show up in your life, and you have a choice in using them. This is where your journey begins in diving into exploring where you are in each of the four relationships that make up your full experience of being a human being. And if there is one relationship that you don't feel connection with, just like the place you sit now, the connection is there—whether you feel it is or you don't. That is a part of the oneness that you can't get away from, even in the face of disconnect.

## The Four Relationships and You

It was many years ago, in my late twenties, that the view of our having *four relationships* came into my mind. It likely started as one of my random contemplations that I followed down the rabbit hole. When it came to me in my knowingness, it just made sense, so the notion stuck. I could reason that within these four specific areas *all* was included because together the four encompassed any relationship we could ever have. It wasn't anything that I shared with anyone or talked about, it was just an awareness stored within me.

When Corey passed away and I became unemployed, I was so lost. I felt like there was no ground underneath me to move forward on. I had hopes but no solid direction. I had applied to get into a dental assisting program but was waiting to hear if I would actually be accepted or not. In the space of having some open time, I felt life press against me in uncertainty and angst. I was searching for the reasons why and searching for purpose, and the words in my head were pushing at me to: *Do something with yourself. Don't just sit there and do nothing. Make this time count for something. Don't let Corey's death be in vain. Don't let Corey's death be for nothing. Take something from this time and make good out of it in honor of him. Live enough life for the both of us now.*

I knew if I didn't do something, I would later regret that I just let this time pass by. So, I decided to put myself to work and begin a project that had been in the back of my mind to do someday: I started to write a book. At first, I didn't know if it was just going to be therapeutic for me, or if I was actually really writing a book. But the more I got into it, the more it felt like it was not just for me but was meant to be shared. As I continued to write, making good use of this time, this pain, and this experience, the four relationships came up within me and wanted to be a part of my story and a part of what is offered to you. So, it is from this space of living and learning, from taking the time to give each of these four relationships attention through my own experiences, that I can lend you insight. To remedy the problems of disconnect and dividedness that can come out of life circumstance, you must use the medicine of connection through each of the four relationships that make up your wholeness. The four relationships are with yourself, others, the earth, and God. They are yours personally and ours globally. These four relationships are the master areas in which connection can become like medicine in your life.

It's time to get a clear view of where you are in each of the four relationships. You are going to rate where you fall on a scale of feeling connected to yourself, others, God, and the earth. In your journal, draw the four lines illustrated below. Make a mark on each line indicating where you would rate your level of connection today. Write your percentage above it and today's date. For example, 0 would be if you feel *completely disconnected*, 25 percent on the line is *mostly disconnected*, 50 percent would be if you feel *sometimes disconnected/sometimes connected*, 75 percent is *mostly connected*, and 100 percent is *fully connected*.

Self    0%————————————— 50% —————————————100%

Others  0%————————————— 50% —————————————100%

God     0%————————————— 50% —————————————100%

Earth   0%————————————— 50% —————————————100%

## The Four Relationships and Duality

Duality also shows up in the four relationships. There is a clear distinction from what sets two apart—for instance, the duality between God and earth, God as Creator spirit and the earth as the physical creation; heaven and earth, if you will, or the non-physical and the physical. There is also a dualistic relationship between self and others: the self as a sort of inner, mental world and others existing in an outer, emotional world.

You will notice that I am simplistically categorizing the dualistic relationships also into four dimensions of physical, emotional, mental, and spiritual—however each is much more dynamic than this. We will get deeper into this, but I want to plant a seed here to show you that these are the same attributes we possess that make up our individual wholeness. Every human being is all four things: physical, spiritual, mental, and emotional. This points to a bigger truth that each of the four relationships together also make up wholeness, even in their dualistic nature. Although it is easy to see the clear distinction and separation between two, such as God and the earth, self and others, the dynamic is still integrally connected.

## The Four Relationships and Multidimensionality

So, the four relationships make up the wholeness of life, and there are also four dimensions of being that make up the wholeness of you. As touched upon, the multiple dimensions of your personal experience are the areas of functioning mentally, emotionally, physically, and spiritually. There is integrated connectedness between these dimensions of body, mind, emotion, and spirit; the currency of which, that can be relationally exchanged between them all, is *energy*.

Energy is energy no matter if it is in a mental, emotional, physical, or non-physical form. For example, mental energy could be thoughts and ideas to develop invention and creation. Emotional energy could be having compassion that comforts another in distress. An example of physical energy is food that is broken down to energize you. And an example of non-physical or spiritual energy is magnetism—non-visible energy that has a physical effect through the attraction of magnetic fields. This is also known as the law of attraction, more commonly called *chemistry* in relationships. Through these examples, you can see that energy can be changed or transferred from one entity to another.

Energy is relational and connective in nature. Energy is also everywhere and in everything. Think of energy as a *holographic coin* of oneness in the fullness of the coin are the integrated multidimensions of mind, emotion, physical, and spiritual. Depending on which side the coin is flipped to there is also either disconnect or connect influencing them. Since, *all* is connected, the impact is on the whole not only in one individual dimension. But because you can easily separate them through categorizing bits and pieces of your human experience, they can become a source of disconnect alongside being a source of connection. It is in their connectedness, however, that you will come to see how they are layered into having a more integrated experience. This awareness will emerge as you explore within yourself—the four relationships. In your self-journey you will increasingly build on how to develop awareness and connection in each of the four relationships so that they can become greater supports for you as you navigate your life in its beautiful fullness.

If you have awareness and actively build up the area of relationship that is weak, it will ultimately have an overall positive affect on you because nothing is absolute. Nothing moves in a vacuum. There is always a ripple effect to some degree, affecting how you are on every level.

## Expanding in Relationship

As I grew and developed from youth into adulthood, relationship continued to change for me. As I matured, my relationships were able to mature too, and I found myself in a new space and ready for a new beginning.

In the summer following my high school graduation, I felt wild and free. Nothing was holding me back and the wind was in my sails. The world was wide-open to me. Two girlfriends and I planned a trip to Cadott, Wisconsin, to attend a music festival called Rock Fest. One hot July morning, we loaded a tent, some food, and our duffle bags full of clothes into my friend Maxine's car and were off down the road, singing as we went. In one day, we traveled twelve hours. Our route was north from central Michigan over the Mackinac Bridge, where our tires hummed as we passed over its metal grates. I looked down, mesmerized by how I could see the water through the bridge as we drove, trusting the road to carry us as we went. From there, we crossed into the Upper Peninsula of Michigan and drove the coastline until we entered Wisconsin for the first time in my life. The hills grew larger and the rolling slopes more beautiful. Then, finally, our destination: "Cadott, Cadott, the land we love to rock."

It was dark and we were tired when we arrived at our campsite. We unloaded the car and slowly worked on pitching the tent. I paused for a moment and leaned against the car, tilting my head back to see the Wisconsin sky above.

"Oh my gosh, look at the sky," I said.

Above us were the northern lights in a complete 360-degree aurora borealis. It danced gorgeously, like rolling white plumes of smoke billowing up to the heavens. I was in awe. Head cranked back and heart burst open, I smiled back at God for the beauty he had created. Little did I know more beauty was to be created in the days to come.

On the start of the four-day festival, I met a tall, gorgeous, dark-haired, green-eyed twenty-four-year-old man from Wisconsin who would become my husband, Corey. The first night he tried to dance with me, but I was hesitant about being too friendly with him. Later in the night, when he and I got separated from my friends in the 'This Bud's for You' beer garden, I nervously said: "We better head back to the campsite." I was not too sure about making a connection with this stranger; but on our walk to find my friends, he made a comment that struck me. He looked over at me as we walked. Our eyes met as the soft smile on his lips gave me a clue as to what his heart might be feeling, and he said, "I bet you get away with a lot."

When he said that, I smiled at him but looked down at the ground a little surprised. I thought to myself, *you don't even know me, how could you say that?* It felt like a statement that only someone who knew me could say, not a complete stranger like he was. But it grabbed my attention because . . . he was right. I did have a sort of fly-under-the-radar quality and had done plenty that might have gotten me in trouble. Something about him saying that made me feel like he already knew me. It caught me off-guard and made me feel a little more comfortable walking in this strange place with someone I had just met.

The next morning, my girlfriends and I were standing by the car when Corey and his buddy walked by. They stopped to talk, his friend being chattier than Corey. Corey listened a moment then turned and walked away. It was in that moment that I had a jolt of waking up to my life. I felt an energetic bolt of lightning shoot through me from above, followed by a thought: *I have to get this guy's attention.* This was unexpected and a little shocking too. I had never had something like that happen before, or since. But in that instant, I understood loud and clear that I was supposed to go after him. And I knew to follow my instinct. By listening to that nudge from God, myself, and the orchestration of life aligning, the rest of the weekend was spent in song, dance, and laughter as we connected as two people destined to become one.

On the second evening of the festival, we found ourselves alone again at the end of the night. This time he laid a blanket down in the grass so that we could lay next to each other and look up at the stars. As we did so, a small, white blaze shot across the night sky above us.

"A shooting star," I said. "Make a wish."

He put his arm around me and pulled me in close, softly saying, "I already did."

He was forward but genuine, putting himself out there to a girl he hadn't even kissed yet. Opening his heart to feel something unexpected and, at the same time, my heart opening too to feel that unexpected stirring of this golden surprise.

By the third night, we stood on the grassy slope to the right of the stage among the crowd of people filling the concert grounds. He looked at me and I was done—at the same time we were just getting started. Then he held me close in his arms and gently swayed me side to side in his smooth lead. His cheek rested against the side of my head as he sang into my ear. The sound of the band Journey singing "Open Arms" rang out from the stage, giving him the words to say as he lulled my heart:

"So, now I come to you with open arms,

Nothing to hide, believe what I say.

So, here I am, with open arms,

Hoping you'll see what your love means to me,

Open arms."

We had only just met, but something bigger than us knew we were supposed to be connected, to be in close relationship with each other, for the sake of love. That surprise connection set forth a beautiful ripple effect that still echoes through my life today. You just never know what beauty lies in building relationship and what love is held there waiting for you, with open arms.

This experience of meeting Corey opened me to being willing to start a new relationship. Even with a complete stranger whom I had no connection with and no guarantee I would ever see again in my life. It opened me to be willing to take the dare to live. To live in connection to myself, taking those subtle cues that moved within me and letting them be the wisdom to not let the moment pass me by. To live in connection to others, taking the time to let someone new get to know me, and I them. To live in connection to the earth, in taking in her layers of gorgeous earthly goodies—like live music and long Wisconsin drives and a place to lay your head at night no matter where you are. And, to live in connection to God, in knowing some things can only be orchestrated by him. Believing that the beauty of what he can create is endless. No matter what stretch of winding path you may be on, a welcome surprise could be only just around the corner. Are you open and listening to life so that you don't miss it? Your chance is now. Be open and let life lead you in this, your dance, to becoming more fully connected in the relationships of your life.

2

# LIFE SPEAKS TO YOU

## Language as the Way of Your World

We speak not only from our lips

Our body sings a song.

We listen not only from our ears,

The heart too can hear what's wrong.

I was recently at lunch with a group and got seated next to a woman who I didn't know well. As we waited for our food to arrive, we turned towards each other and began talking. The conversation got heavy quickly as she expressed her condolences: "I was so sorry to hear about the passing of your husband. What happened?"

I hesitated a moment, checking in with myself to see if I was feeling okay enough to dive into that dark, deep-end of my life with a near stranger. I gauged my safety to do so in a second by how my body responded to her question. I did not tighten up in my chest or hold my breath at the invitation to share. I felt steady and calm. I felt I was safe to plunge into the deep end with openness through sharing instead of closing down in an inner shutter. I opened my mouth to speak and felt strength in my voice and heard evenness in its tone. Sometimes the hard stuff can come out so matter-of-fact, even though the tears and the horror are not far under the surface.

I began with how Corey had been sick for a couple of weeks, taking cold medicine and going to bed early, but his breathing had been getting more labored and the medicine wasn't doing enough. When he finally went in to see the doctor, they discovered that he was battling pneumonia. It had advanced to the point that one of his lungs had collapsed due to fluid built up around it. I told her, "When they were draining the fluid off, they ended up puncturing his lung and then the force with which the lung expanded was so sudden and violent, it caused more damage and inflammation." I explained how these complications added stress to his body and weakened his lung's strength for recovery. "He was in the hospital for thirty-three days and was due to come home on Friday, but ended up having a heart attack on Wednesday," I continued. "I feel like his body was working so hard to breathe." With tears now coming to my eyes from the abyss of my grief, I said, "He was working so hard to get home to us, but with all that he was up against it was taking a toll on his heart, and maybe that is why he had a heart attack right at the end."

She looked at me with sadness drooping her eyes and replied, "Aww, his heart was taxed from the stress put on his lungs. I am so sorry he didn't make it." We talked for another moment about having to trust that when it's your time, it's your time, and that as hard as my husband was fighting to get home to the kids and I, and as hard as his heart was fighting to get the flow of oxygen to his body, there were unforeseen events that made this the way it was to be.

In my openness with her, she then reflected back and shared openly with me. "You know, I had a scare not that long ago," she began. She shared how she had been having awful back pain and that she just kept pushing through it until a nurse friend said, "Pain is not normal. Your body is telling you something is wrong. You need to see a doctor."

She took the advice of her friend and found out that she had a tumor growing on her ovary. "Thankfully," she said, "the tumor was benign and they were able to remove it. And you know what? Ever since my surgery, my back pain has gone away. It was being caused by the tumor, and I never would have known about the tumor if I hadn't had the back pain."

Looking back at our brief conversation, I see how the simple moment held space for sharing experience and wisdom. Not direct, intentional wisdom, but wisdom in hearing between the lines of what the stories shared. The wisdom of awareness that our *body* speaks to us. It was that subtle language that was going on for me as I checked in with how my body felt to know if it was an emotionally safe time for me to talk. And in her story, her body had talked to her through very obvious pain, telling her that something was wrong. For my husband too, his body told him with worsening symptoms, despite the medicine, that he needed to see his doctor and that the situation was bigger than what he could handle on his own.

## Layers of Language

There is an unspoken dimension that gets communicated along with the things that you say. Likewise, there are subtleties that you can pick up on that go beyond the words that you hear. This is because language is much more than just the spoken or written word. Language is the way of the world. It's how life speaks to you—not just other people speaking to you, but *life itself* speaking to you. Your life is speaking to you, but you might not be listening. In disconnection to yourself or to things in your life, you may have turned off your ability to hear the deeper language, and with it, its deeper truth. But being able to hear the layers of language is imperative for being able to navigate your way.

The ability to hear both the subtle and obvious layers of language is humanity's built-in navigation system and human beings are the wiser for having it. It is both intuitive and literal, and you need *both* means of interpreting to navigate well. When you can attune to the fact that language comes to you across many different receptors, you get a fuller understanding of what is being said. Language comes to you through words, but also through movement, emotion, the timing of things, even synchronicities. Language speaks to you in a feeling, a thought, or sometimes in an indescribable sense. Sometimes language is loud and obvious, and sometimes it takes the skill of listening between the lines of subtlety to hear it.

## It's Time to Start Paying Attention

How many people in the world do you think are too busy to pay attention to things in their life that are calling out to them, "LOOK AT ME," "NOTICE ME," or, "DO SOMETHING ABOUT ME."

What in your life is calling out to you to *pay attention?* Maybe you are noticing pain in your body or emotional pain. Or perhaps there is pain in your thoughts and memories, or the pain of feeling spiritually despondent. The pain is saying something to you. It is there because it needs to be listened to. Are you listening to what your pain is saying? Listen and seek to understand the pain and then support it—find the support you need so that you can attend to the pain.

Pain can be sharply intense, or it can show up as mere discomfort. It can even creep in over time so that you barely notice that it is there unless you take the time to look. This is not just about your body, it is about your place in life and how you are in it. It might be about your career, your living situation, your relationship with yourself or with someone else. Ask yourself: *what am I pushing to the side and not paying attention to? What areas in life are causing me pain or discomfort?* Take a moment to jot down in your journal the first thoughts that come to mind.

Some people might answer that they have a habit of continually sacrificing themselves at home, at work, or in the community to the detriment of their health. With this, discomfort shows up in physical and mental fatigue. Other people may identify with putting all of their time into projects, personal interests, and advancing in life, while important relationships with the people in their lives are disregarded and taken for granted. This discomfort shows up in the arguments and hurt feelings with the people who are left feeling unimportant. And others can see themselves in the pattern of forgetting to stop and enjoy moments because they are too caught up in emotional drama that tends to consume them. In that pain, not only is drama wound tight around mental, emotional, and physical stress, it also spreads sideways into other relationships and environments. Or consider a person who has an understanding of what God means to them but does not have a relationship with God that feels personal and accessible. The discomfort here is showing up in feeling a spiritual gap, as if they are somehow left out of mattering in life. Maybe they even notice how others seem to have this connection and yet they wonder, *Where is God for me?*

It comes to be that the things left unnoticed in your life are the things that should have been catching your attention all along. Pain pops up as a disruption, calling you to pay attention to what else is going on. The thing that you are not noticing well enough is a side-effect from your being disconnected on some level from God, yourself, others, or the earth. Maybe you are disconnected from seeing the beauty of the earth and its people because of the dramas of life. Or you are disconnected from taking into consideration your body that carries you along for the ride, not giving it the value God intended. There is a real possibility that there is something that you are not paying attention to, which is why the pain and discomfort keep repeating in a cycle. Simply placing your attention on where your pain-points are in life can be helpful for seeing where inattention may be creating turbulence. Look at your written list of pain-points and think what it could be that you may not be hearing in these areas of your life. In identifying pain and beginning to pay attention to what your behavior is in relationship to it, you can start to uncover where your issues of disconnect are. Often, we are so engrossed in what is front and center, that that which is on the side gets overlooked.

### When You Listen, Life Can Be Heard

Life is speaking to you in a language that is decipherable in diverse ways, so if you aren't listening fully, you're missing pieces. It's like looking at a fifty-piece puzzle with five pieces missing—the whole of it is not seen without *all* of the pieces in place, completing the picture. You have gaps in how you are living. Holes that you can fill with awareness and connection. You can probably feel these gaps. They show up in dissatisfaction, burnout, struggle, anger, and a feeling of giving up. They are evidence that you have disconnect somewhere in your life.

The first step towards solution is to take the time to diversify what *"language"* means to you and to grow your ability to hear the language of your life, to better comprehend its nature. You must be open to learn but also *to play* with developing your awareness to receive what life is saying to you. I say *play* because look at a child in play: they are open and engaged with the moment. They are not analyzing or overthinking as we adults do. So, it is helpful to approach the activities I will be sharing with you with a curious, child-like openness. As your understanding of life's language expands, you become better equipped to live a fuller life. This does not equate to life not being challenging anymore; it means you have more connected support in navigating it.

Think of it this way: the more information you have about something and the more angles you can see it from, the easier it is to understand and work with. When you are listening with your eyes, ears, senses, intuition, body, mind, heart, and soul, just think how full of an experience that is. All the puzzle pieces come into view: the picture is seen in its fullness. Life comes alive in the many ways it can reach you. Like all the different colors in the puzzle's picture make it what it is, all the colors in the language of life make it what it can be.

## Life Speaks in Many Ways

I was talking to a friend recently about the journey of writing this book. I confided in her that it has not been an easy process and that it is a lot of work, especially in my heavy grieving, and that I would kind of like to just be finished with it. "What was I thinking?" I said to her. "While going through the hardest thing I have ever gone through in my life—losing Corey—I decide to do one of the hardest things I've ever done: writing this book." But then I said, "Writing a book *someday* has been something I have felt in myself for a long time, and maybe now is just the right time."

My friend replied, "Oh, I just got goosebumps."

To which I thought to myself internally, *Yes, okay God, I'll keep going with this hard work you have given me.* Her goosebumps were an attention-grabbing signal from outside of myself, confirming my instinct to keep listening to that inner inkling that urged me to not give up on this endeavor. Goosebumps are like truth-detecting alarms going off when they pop up on your skin. There is a spiritual communication that is happening through goosebumps: they give you physical feedback from the spiritual realm to take notice of what was just said, giving you encouragement that you are on the right track and that there is truth in what has been spoken. In this case, it was her goosebumps confirming my truth.

Another time when life spoke to me in more directive clues was in the early years of building a business as an energy therapist. I was sitting in the waiting room at our local medical center waiting to be called back for my mammogram. It's never the most comfortable experience to have your boob smashed into a pancake, so I was trying to distract myself by letting my eyes wander around the waiting area. I noticed a placard hanging on one of the walls across from me with the heading "Women's Wednesdays." This drew my attention, but the rest was too small to read from where I was, so I stood up from my seat and walked over to read it. It advertised that once a month on a Wednesday, women who come in for their mammogram would be treated to a complimentary chair massage. This sounded great, and I immediately wished I had known this ahead of time to schedule my own mammo on that day. *How cool that they are offering free massage in support of women's health*, I thought. Then I thought, *Hmmm, I wonder if they might be interested in also offering energy therapy?*

As I stood staring at the advertisement on the wall, my name was called and I was taken back to the imaging suite. As I walked with the woman who would be doing my mammogram, I asked her about Women's Wednesday massages and told her that I did energy therapy and was curious if that might be something they would like to offer complimentary on their Wednesdays as well. She was able to give me the name of the woman who oversaw this program and told me I could check with her. In a matter of five short minutes, a seed was planted, an action was taken, and a connection was made, opening a door to the future. My future. Funny how life does that sometimes—puts you where you need to be in the moment you should be there.

I didn't end up offering my services at Women's Wednesdays, but I did make that call. And I am so glad that I did because that call opened up a conversation for me to be considered instead for offering complimentary sessions to their staff as a wellness perk. Which then later led to me being able to teach meditation at their facility for community members. And all of this eventually brought me to the place of being asked if I would like to be a part of the Integrative Health Department they were in the process of forming. *Umm, yes! And holy cow, really!?* I had the privilege of being part of the founding of the Integrative Health Department and worked there for seven great years. In fact, I had been their longest active provider in the department when I resigned several months after the loss of my husband. Sometimes I wish I was still there, but life changes, and moves us, and we must be willing to move with life. This is again where listening and hearing the language spoken to you through the intricacies of your life gives you a direction that will support you in getting to where you are meant to be.

Life can speak to you audibly and visually, in synchronicities, in signs, symbols, and nudges, and in goosebumps signaling you to pay attention. Life speaks to you in the way things land on your heart. And it speaks to you when you notice how things *don't* land on your heart. By building a larger language base of what can be communicated to you when you are immersed in living, you can actually feel a fuller, more heart-centered connection to your life. It can become easier to make life decisions because you're not doing it in the two-tone grays and whites of just seeing and hearing. Through listening with your body, mind, heart, and soul, you are being fully aware and engaged with life. You are doing it in full color, bringing in the whole palette of the multiple dimensions of human experience. You are living connected into your unique path in life that only *you* are meant to walk, for yourself, and for others. You are living in your imperfection and in your goodness—both of colorful, whole purpose.

## Changing How to Look at What Language Is

Because connection is facilitated through the use of language, language is a necessary area to touch upon as you journey towards being able to connect adequately enough so that your relationships can be the supportive medicine in your life that you want them to be. In the dimensions and colors, tones, and shades of expression, both the subtle and the obvious are present as a lucid language. This spreads throughout the channels of communication and translates into *meaning*. This is why it is important to understand that language goes far beyond the spoken word.

In the last chapter, the groundwork was laid for seeing that relationships contain elements of unity, duality, and multidimensionality. Just like relationship, language is also an expression of oneness, duality, and multidimensionality all rolled up into one. Language is an expression of oneness in that it is but one thing: a means to relatable connection. Language is an expression of duality in the yin-yang nature of communication: a sender sending and a receiver receiving. Two roles make up the one thing. And language is multidimensional through its diversity. This can be seen in the fact that there are many variations of language among human beings— approximately 6,500 languages are spoken in the world today. Diversity is prominent in language, but to have an expanded understanding of language as not being limited to just the spoken or written dimension, you have to look further than the obvious.

The diversity of language as multidimensional is held in a much broader communication system that permeates all. Because language is everywhere, and in everything. The language of the mind is mental. The language of emotions is emotional. The language of the body is physical. And the language of spirit is spiritual. However, these four are not separate. They interrelate and integrate together into the wholeness of experiencing.

In the death of my husband, I could feel the depth of my loss in the sharp, physical pain stabbing at my heart, in the drowning wave of emotional sadness, in the spiritual absence of his soul being gone from his body, and in the screaming, mental anguish of realizing that he was never coming back.

This language of grief I understand all too well. At times I still hear and feel every part of it, and all at once, when the emotional waves of feeling bring it in close to me.

A lighter example of the integration of these layers of language is in watching my children play sports. Physically, my attention is honed into watching them compete. Emotions roll with the highs and lows of the game. Spiritually, I value the growth and character-building that being on a team is teaching them. And mentally, and sometimes verbally, I am their biggest cheerleader.

Do you have a personal situation you can think back to now in order to see how each of these four ways of experiencing was heard within you? Maybe a moment of stress, for example. Take time to write down your situation. Try to put a few words to how that experience affected you physically, mentally, emotionally, and spiritually.

To further dissect the integration of the dimensions of language, imagine yourself in the following situation: think about sitting down in your favorite café and ordering a pastry. It tastes delicious and your brain says, *Mmm, sweet*, as you enjoy your second bite. There is a physical communication between your taste buds and your brain as your mouth takes in the food and your brain deciphers it and elicits a pleasurable emotion. This is a type of language.

Now think about what happens when you are standing in a busy crowd, cell phones all around you, and you use yours to call a friend who lives 2,000 miles away. How is this possible? There is no physical connection between you and your friend, and yet there is a language between your phones that enables them to accurately tap into each other so that you can connect to your friend in an instant. Distance is no boundary here as the language of your cell phone is transmitted across the world with towers and signals and energy conversion—a language of expansive connection all its own.

There is also a natural, earthly language between a buzzing honey bee flying through a garden and the loudly bright orange lily that it is instinctively drawn to. There is a mental language as you dialogue with yourself internally, *What should I wear today, the black or blue shirt?* And there is an emotional language at play when a child tells you, "I'm fine," but you intuit by the way they are holding their body—arms stiffly crossed across their chest, eyes darting away from you as you look at them—that they are anything but fine. Yes, language is multidimensional. Streams of connected communication ping between sender and receiver across mental and emotional, physical, and non-physical, natural and spiritual dimensions—and all at the same time.

## The Interconnection of Language Information

The first time that I was really exposed to the reality of language being multidimensional in such a way that it began to sink in as a usable tool, I was in my first ever Intuition Thursday class in 2007. About eight other women and I were sitting in a small coffee shop that was part of an alternative therapy clinic. I only knew one person there, my neighbor and new friend, Elise, who had invited me to go with her. Our teacher was Annette Bruchu, an expert in intuition and energy. I would come to find out that Annette was very gifted in leading her students to discover parts of themselves they didn't know were there through enabling us to have experiences that were multisensory and multidimensional. We were like little birdies curious to learn how to fly and she the mama bird, nudging us along in our own growth, until we discovered we really could soar.

We came to the part in the evening where Annette opened the floor for questions. She explained that we would go around the room and everyone could ask a question of the group, to which anyone in the group could share what intuitive impressions they were receiving in response to the inquiry. *What?* I thought, *I can't do that.* I did already have an understanding from my life experience that sometimes God could reach out and speak to me, and I could hear him, but I didn't know how I could possibly hear anything for anybody else—and on command. I was very nervous because I knew I was supposed to participate and, at the same time, I was a complete fish out of water, out of my own element... or so I thought.

Being the newest to the group that night, I was allowed to ask my question first. I asked about my mom who had, at that time, been gone for six years. "Is my mom, Diane, ever able to be around me?" The responses that I got from the circle of women were beyond worth the discomfort of knowing that I would have to reciprocate next. I heard that, yes, she was around me and around my infant son a lot. I heard that she loved watching me with him and was proud, seeing that I was a good mom. This information came through in feelings, impressions, emotions, and images that touched the other women in the room as open and connected vessels of communication.

Annette gave insight too, sharing, "I can see pink around you. Your mom is here with you now. And she's very proud of you. I see her handing a rose out to you. She wants to give you this rose. It is her love that she is sending to you now." I cried, I was so deeply touched. Not only was my mom present in this very moment, but she was able to communicate through all of these amazing women, and I was able to hear her through them. This was life-changing. In this moment, I knew I wanted to learn to connect better to her *myself* so that I too could have open communication for our ongoing relationship.

Next, it was my turn to be on the giving end for someone else's question. *Gulp.* I was so nervous I was shaking a bit in my seat. I had no idea what I was doing or how to make anything of the sort happen. Everything intuitive I had previously experienced had been organic, not facilitated. But I was willing to try.

It was Nellie's turn to ask her question. She had a person that she wanted to check in on. Annette had her say the person's name so that we all could tap into his specific energy. Then we were all instructed: "Close your eyes, focus on your breath, and draw your attention inward. Pay attention to any impressions that come to you." Still shaking in my seat, I did just that. I closed my eyes, felt my breath, and centered inward.

And then a strange and random image popped into my mind's eye. A seahorse. I could see it plain as day. It was a pretty greenish blue and its tail was wrapped around a piece of seaweed. It appeared to be just hanging on and hanging out. *What the heck?* I thought. *This is nonsense. A seahorse? That doesn't even mean anything. How am I going to share this with the room when everyone else is sharing such beautiful, meaningful information?* As the sharing went around the room, I sunk into my seat. My throat felt tight, pinched off from my fear of sharing such a silly response.

"Korinn, what did you get?" Annette asked. I could have said nothing, and had wanted to a little bit. But I let honesty and bravery be stronger than the doubt in myself in that moment. I opened my mouth with a look of *I know this is ridiculous* on my face and said, "I saw a seahorse." Annette asked for a bit more detail, so I shared its color and what it was doing.

What happened next shocked me. Nellie pulled out a book from the bag sitting beside her on the floor. It was titled *Animal Spirit Guides*, by Steven Farmer. She said, "Let me see what seahorse means." *What?* I thought to myself, *Animals have meanings and there's a book on this?* I was flabbergasted. Not only was my seeing a seahorse an actual intuitive impression received on command, but it actually had a meaning. She sat with the book in her lap and read out loud "You're being called upon to sacrifice your own needs at this time to be in service to another person or cause." She smiled and said, "Well, that sounds like me in the situation." Then she read on silently, and said, "Hmm, this meaning sounds more like him." As she read, "You're about to go on a quest or spiritual pilgrimage of some sort, so prepare yourself by being open to the opportunity when it surfaces." Then Nellie shared a little bit more about her person in question. He was someone that she was in a caregiver role with. She felt like he was getting close to it being his time to crossover, but she wanted to check if her intuitive hunch could be confirmed. I too could see how the book's message of seahorse could apply to what she was describing, how she was "in service" and how his "spiritual pilgrimage" could be the approach of his end on earth. I was floored.

Not only did I learn there was a decipherable language in animal energy and symbolism, but that I could quiet myself, ask a question inwardly, and receive impressions that were meaningful in response. I immediately remembered back to all the times as a teen when I would be falling asleep in my bed, with my eyes closed, but I would be seeing strange and random pictures flash before me. A dog, a face, the color red, a birdhouse on a tree, and so on. They meant nothing to me. Just some weird thing that happened sometimes that I assumed must be normal. But what I was beginning to understand about myself in this moment was that it had been my *spirit sight* in natural action. And I was now embarking on a journey of self-discovery in learning how to use it as a tool for connection because it is a natural part of how God has made me, with an ability to be a seer, a visionary. Spiritual communication didn't need to be something that I hoped would happen to me anymore. It was something I was realizing that I could actively participate in, just like any other form of communication.

To simplify this, think of language as exchangeable energy that *is* connectivity. It is like there are imaginary lines of connection through which communication constantly flows—an interconnected highway of language information. Language enables you to receive and perceive the signals being sent. Like that bright orange color of the tiger lily, mentioned earlier, which is signaling, "Well, hello there, honey bee. Land here so earth can grow more beautiful flowers like me." And the closed body language of the child signaling: "I am not okay, but I am not open to talk with you about it right now." Also, my personal examples of connecting in spirit. In every language, we have to cultivate an ability to see beyond the obvious and read between the lines. That takes a lot more than just being able to speak and hear to do so.

Fortunately, people are naturally built for this exchange of language information. You are naturally able to integrate and synthesize multi-informational input and make sense of it. In science, this is called *physiology of information theory*, when sensory information is taken in as input from the environment and deciphered within the nervous system. It's like the cell phone analogy: one piece of language is transported, transformed, and then received as decipherable on the other end. Britannica.com states: "The human body sends 11 million bits per second to the brain for processing, yet the conscious mind seems to be able to process only 50 bits per second. It appears that a tremendous amount of compression is taking place if 11 million bits are being reduced to less than 50." Wow, right? We are remarkable.

People are multisensory beings in a multidimensional world. We all have the five senses and the subtle senses, too. All of us. The five senses are touch, taste, sight, smell, and hearing. The subtle senses are emotive feeling, cognitive knowing, intuitive sensing, and spiritual feeling. You are able to put together and perceive with all of these built-in abilities that decipher the multitude of input coming into you from your life. And this happens simply in the miracle of being. Perception of language is multisensorial, too. All of these facets integrate into your interpretation, which then translates into your output—spreading across mind, body, emotion, and spirit in your reaction. You are constantly immersed in the steady flow of the input and output of information. What is external comes in as input and what is internal goes out as output.

Think about a time when someone did something that made you angry. As this thing occurred outside of you, you took in the reality through your senses, ears and eyes, and heart. Have you ever been so angry that you yelled at the person or situation? Me too. An instant burst of hot-faced, verbal ammo unleashed towards the provoking victim. Coming unleashed in anger is a perfect example of how you feel on the inside making a dramatic exit. Is not mind, body, emotion, and spirit all wrapped up into this flowing exchange from outside to in, from inside to out? They move together as one, though they are different in and of themselves.

## Awareness Exercise

In doing this exercise, you will be playing with experiencing what shows up as integrated through external perception and then through a moment of internal perception.

○ First, look around and allow yourself to be aware of all of the varying bits of information through your *outer awareness*. As you do so, take in what you see, hear, smell, touch, and feel. But also watch where your mind goes and notice how you feel emotionally or spiritually because of it.

○   Now, close your eyes, but keep being an open observer, this time through your *inner awareness*. Take in the perceivable bits about how you are inside of yourself in this moment.

Now that you have observed watching both inside and outside of yourself in different ways, think about what you noticed all together. Maybe you noticed the color in the room, temperature of air, or a sound in the background. Maybe you noticed body sensation, like hunger or ache, a mental thought passing through as you commented to yourself. Maybe you noticed you felt tired or peaceful, curious or hopeful. So much of what comes up for us, moment to moment, we don't usually notice.

## The Eyes of Perception

In any given moment, your attention could be pulled in many different directions because there is a seemingly endless number of things for you to perceive. Sometimes people miss seeing something because of where their focus is. So, it ends up being that what you perceive, and even how you perceive, is affected by the eyes through which you see. Is the glass half-empty or half-full type of thing? Do you see through eyes of love or eyes of fear and hate? What is your overall tone as you walk into a situation? Are you open or closed?

Because language is a connective energy that permeates everything, there is a general *effect* that it has. Language sent or received promotes either openness, like love, or closedness, like fear and hate. How you are affects both the messages you send *and* how you receive messages. As you shift to being open or closed, your whole personal energy shifts, which can color your perspective and experience according to whether you are in connection with the language of love or the language of hate and fear. There is an energy exchange here, since language is a form of energy.

## Awareness Exercise

Here is an energy exercise that I learned in my energy medicine studies that will give you insight through direct experience. It demonstrates how energy permeates your being and affects what you perceive. First, read through the bulleted steps and then go back and do the exercise. Pay attention to how you feel as you do this.

o   Stand up.

o   Think of something or someone you love, maybe even smile about it or them.

o   Next, jump up and down several times and notice how it feels.

o   Now think of something or someone who makes you feel angry.

o   Jump up and down again several times and notice how it feels.

o   Go back to thinking about the thing that you love, with a smile.

o   Now jump up and down.

o   Finally, reflect on how it felt when you were jumping engaged with the feeling love *vs.* when you were feeling hateful anger. In doing this, some people notice that their body felt heavier with hate—that it seemed to take more effort to jump. Also, maybe you noticed it was easier to jump and you felt lighter when you were in a state of love. By thinking specific thoughts, you become immersed in its corresponding energy.

Now, here is another energy experiencing exercise for you:

o   Notice how it feels in your body when you say the word *love*. Say it out loud or in your mind and notice how you feel saying it.

o   Now, notice how it feels when you say the word *fear*.

o   How does it feel when you say *hate*?

o   Some people notice that their body feels more relaxed or open when in the energy and the language of love. Maybe you noticed your body felt more tense or closed when you were saying *hate* or *fear* and were immersed in the energy and the language of fear and hate.

## The Link Between How You Are and What You Perceive

In each of those exercises, you were able to experience an awareness of how you were in relation to memories and also simple spoken words. You were able to experience how these had an effect on you that stretched further than just being in the mind as thoughts. They rippled out through you and colored *how you were* in the moment. The fact that you were changed by simple and subtle things, can open your understanding that *what* you are perceiving permeates through the integrated layers of how you perceive and thus how you are. The thoughts you think and the feelings you feel are simultaneously integrated into your physical and subtle experience. Your whole self is responding to language in even the tiniest of shifts, like saying the word *love*, or sometimes in big shifts like being overcome with anger. Emotions don't just live on the emotional plane, and thoughts are not just mental; they also create real, physical energy that impacts your body. This is how words hurt at a deeper level: the body stores the wounds of deeply hurtful words the same as it would store a scar. It might fade with time, but the negative words leave a mark.

During the exercises, your body responded to the energy of language because there is an intertwined synergy between yourself and what you are in relationship with—even down to the relationship you have with the words you speak and the thoughts you have. Language spreads through your whole being because it is connective energy. You are both immersed in a continual sea of energy and of relationship. And in your relationships, you are either moving in a direction of openness or closedness.

## Learning to Hear and See

When I was a teenager, my friends and I would cruise around in cars on the weekends. We'd slowly creep down backroads, gravel crunching under tires with dust billowing up behind us. I can still smell the dust of those worn dirt roads. Sometimes I'd lose the call for "shotgun" and have to sit in the back seat. With Guns and Roses, Steve Miller Band, or Creedence Clearwater Revival playing through the rear speaker into my ear, I'd look out the window as we drove and watch the trees outside. They came alive to me; they danced and moved. I could feel their energy pressing their beauty into the wonder of my mind. I felt a kinship to the trees, as if we were somehow connected—as they'd been ever-present beings in my life. I had loved them as a little kid, too, for the fun and adventure they offered when I would climb them, but as a teen they took on a more mystical edge. Through my connection with them, I was learning to *hear* in open awareness and to see with eyes that saw beyond the obvious.

One time, again on a dirt back road, I was gifted to see an angel in a constellation of stars. Often, we would stop the car and sit until we saw headlights and someone yelled "car" as a signal to move on down the road. As we sat there, dark night all around us, I looked out the back window, and there she was, cradled by the silhouette of the trees, letting her light shine through to my gaze. Shining on me. The perfect impression of the shape of an angel landed on my heart from the stars. Something in me moved: I had an awareness, a recognition, it was *my* angel. I took ownership in it, felt connection, and welcomed the identification. Ever since that night, that constellation has always been my angel in the sky. When I see it, it makes me smile and makes me feel like I'm not alone. In these organic moments of inner growth and outer discovery, I was learning a new language, spoken by spirit through the natural world. My heart was learning to grow the ears my spirit has always had. Do you believe in angels? Perhaps one has shown itself to you in subtle ways too.

Like sponges in the sea, we soak up the language that is permeating the space we are in and release out the language we are currently composed of. It is as much an energetic exchange as an exchange of physicality and consciousness. There is an unspoken back-and-forth communication, whether or not we are aware of it. And just because we don't have eyes to see it, doesn't mean it is not there. You might only need to begin to learn its language to start to hear its undercurrents being spoken in your life. All the surface stuff can be easy to perceive, but what is under the surface is worth paying attention to. In fact, it could be the key to reaching a sharper focus with your perception, for seeing where you are disconnected and where you are connected. Take a moment and write down the first thoughts and feelings that come to you in answering these questions spontaneously for yourself: do you have a sense of what is being said under the surface of your life? Is there a whisper of something under the day-to-day surface of home or family life? Maybe something good that you don't often see? Is there a hint of something under the surface in your day-to-day personal way of being? Can you hear anything else being said underneath the surface of your life?

## Learning a New Dimension of Language

Things that are tangible and physically clear are naturally easier to be aware of—the color of the wall, the weather outside, the feeling of hunger in your belly. But what about all that is not so blatantly clear? What about the stuff that takes more awareness to learn its language, like someone's mood or mental state? What about the language of the spiritual quality of something, like a location you traveled to, or a book that pulled at you from the shelf, drawing you towards reading it? What about the emotional value of things, like a YouTube video, a handwritten letter, or a shared silence? Some things are left up to interpretation. Some things are left up to your noticing alone for their full impact to land in your life.

Noticing is just the first step. Next, it is knowing how to speak the language so that you can decipher its communication to you. After all, if you are speaking Japanese to me, and I only speak Lakota Sioux, my accuracy of interpretation is going to be pretty poor. Improving one's ability to interpret language is possible, but it takes time, interest, exposure to the language, and practice. And, this always involves trial and error. Just because you don't pick up on the new language straight away does not mean it's not being communicated, and it does not mean that you are incapable of learning. Keep trying. When someone is learning Japanese, they don't expect fluency right off the bat; nor should you expect learning a new language—whether it be a physical, emotional, spiritual, or mental language—to be immediate.

## Awareness Exercise

This is an exercise to practice listening to the language between the lines and to start picking up on subtle things communicated in this very moment. I will start by being the example for you. For me in this moment, I hear wind chimes tinging outside my window as a gentle breeze blows through my flower garden. I pause and I ask, *What are the wind chimes saying to me?* I feel peace. I hear *easy breezy* in my mind. I listen and hear the tick of the grandfather clock on the living room wall. I ask, *What is the ticking clock saying to me?* I understand in my heart and mind simultaneously: *life has a rhythm, a cadence it keeps.* There is a windy sound outside that seems far off. I hear, *What seems far away is closer than you think.* The hum of the highway: *busy, busy, busy.* There is no wrong or right answer—there is only impression and expression. Something in you is there to receive and be aware of the undertones of that which surrounds you. Play with receiving and perceiving.

Now it's your turn.

o   Listen for a sound around you, to feel what is communicated. Note: it may help to close your eyes for inward connection.

o   Pause to ask yourself: What is _____ saying?

o   Pick another sound to focus in on and ask again: What is _____ saying?

o   Now look around you and let something grab your eye's attention.

o   Ask your inner self: What is _____ saying?

o   Repeat again, with another visual cue.

This is a practice of communicating with the world around you with open awareness. Creating a dialogue in which a response is reciprocated from the asking.

## Life-Giving Beauty in Language

Picture a rose in your mind. You can see its vibrant colors, imagine the feel of its soft petals, remember the smell of its sweet scent, and notice its sturdy stem holding up this beholden beauty full of life. But beyond the gorgeous naturalness of the rose, there is a deeper, life-giving beauty to the language with which it is endowed to communicate. What is the rose saying? One nuance of the rose is an expression of love. A visual beauty speaking inaudible preciousness to your heart. When one receives a rose, it tells the tale *you are loved*. This is a love that extends from God as creator of the natural world, creator of the rose. And extends to you through another person in an emotionally driven gesture intended to express their love. However, the rose itself not only expresses love, it inspires it. The rose inspires us to *give it love* through the watering, cultivation, and gentle treatment we give it once it is cut. I am not sure if a rose is a signal of love universally, but if you are familiar with its message of love, then you *understand* its language. But understanding is not just one dimensional; you understand this message mentally, but can you *feel* the message of the rose as well? Can you *feel* its message of love?

How did the rose ever open its heart and give to this world all of its beauty?

It felt the encouragement of light against its being.

—Hafiz

How do you receive this quote? Does it give you a mental image? Does it encourage you to feel any emotion? Or to glimpse a spiritual message between the lines of what is being said? Read it again. Can you feel the light in your heart? How does that feel in your body as the direct and indirect language of it sinks in?

You are receiving information through varying layers of language: inner language, outer language, spiritual language, and sensorial language. Isn't it beautiful to feel the layers of language, that is everywhere and in everything, speaking to you? Isn't it beautiful to brush up against the many ways in which language can connect you and in which your heart, like a rose, can open and grow through these connections?

## Language's Potential for Disconnect

Although language is a great and masterful connector, you must not forget that it can also be a disconnector—at times, moving you further away from what's in your life. There is a double side to it. But remember, even in disconnection, you are still connected; it is actually the connection that amplifies the feeling of being disconnected.

As you interpret signals from the world, you may get confused or have mixed messages. Complexity can weave a tangled web. Language can be tricky—hard to decipher and easy to misconstrue. So, you must try to understand the deeper meaning of language in order to be able to discern it and foster connection. When you don't understand the true voice behind a language, then there are holes in your understanding, and these gaps can foster even more disconnection.

My son and I were out riding bikes together in our neighborhood. He loves biking and was happy to have this time just the two of us. I was enjoying the ride, too. He has a newer mountain bike, while my old ten-speed only has partially functioning gears. Plus, I am older and slower, so I seemed to always be in the rear. We were headed up a hill when I thought to myself, *I am going to push it and try to ride up next to him*. I announced, "I'm coming up on your right," and pedaled a little faster. Then, in a quick sequence of events, he put on his brakes, I bumped into him, and then turned, trying to avoid a full-on crash with him, and flew head-first off of my bike and into the ditch. My arms went out to brace my fall as I awkwardly tried to land as softly as possible. This little bike blooper ended up with both of us getting angry and defensive with each other.

I explained to him my interpretation: "I said, 'I'm coming up on your right,' and then you put on your brakes in front of me."

He saw it differently and argued back, "No, I tapped on my brakes, I didn't slow down, and then you said, 'I'm coming up on your right.'"

After going back and forth, not being able to accept the other's viewpoint, I had to walk away. In our home, we get into arguments like this from time to time. There is a volleying back and forth. "No, I didn't." "Yes, you did." Sound familiar? I can chuckle at the madness of the back-and-forth pattern right now, but in the moment, we were each caught up in being right. Under the surface, the real conversation was not about who was right or wrong, but was about the event of our combined flub and my ditch crash.

I came back to him later and said, "I don't like how it feels when we fight."

He said, "I don't like it either."

Then I suggested, "How about when we get into an argument, instead of deflecting and getting defensive, which only pushes us further apart, we meet in the middle and take responsibility for our part?" Then I said, "I take responsibility for trying to pass too close to you."

He said, "I take responsibility for skidding in front of you."

Between the lines of our verbal argument were the deeper-held feelings. My son didn't want me to get hurt by flying off my bike, but he also didn't want to be the reason for it. And I didn't want to be the idiot who got too close and caused my own mishap. But we were both responsible and, in the end, we could see this.

What we both needed was to take a step towards the other in our disagreement, not to plant our feet and turn our cheek away. You can never come back to connection if you cannot be open to accepting that someone else might have a different view or opinion than you. When you close your ears to genuinely listening and are consumed with blaming, finger-pointing, and deflecting, then there is no way to be in right relationship. Right relationship *is* connecting; its opposite is disconnecting. Language can serve either direction. It has the potential to add to connection with openness or to add to disconnect when your language perpetuates the issue.

So, it can be pivotal to feel into what is needed *under* the surface of a situation to support connection *vs.* perpetuating disconnection. Again, the value is in listening between the lines. Examining this in your relationships can be the difference between asking yourself: *am I listening with my ears or am I listening with my heart?* Contemplate if you are only hearing the words being said in the situation or if you are hearing the emotional, spirit, or human subtleties that are showing up, perhaps in jumbled misunderstanding? In the situation with my son, listening with my ears was hearing that he was stuck in his viewpoint and was *not* seeing mine. Listening with my heart looked like taking a step back to give us both space, and then seeing that I too was adding to the disconnect by being stuck in my mental stance consumed by anger. From there, I allowed myself to soften enough to have an open conversation that brought us closer. It is worth looking at what language needs to happen to work through distance and foster connection.

## Skill in Using Language

My husband's death seems so senseless and is beyond painful. Yet, I cannot argue with where I am. I am in pain *but* still with a hope for my life. I cannot, I do not, let go of hope. And my efforts in keeping my heart open in hope is projected out through words I use to describe where I am. For me, this language has been natural. I feel it in my heart and, because of that, what I say can soothe me. Again and again, I bring myself back to the center of my heart, telling myself words like, *We will never really be apart.* And, *Maybe, there's a bigger reason that I could never understand, but that God understands, of why this had to happen.* It also involves feeling in my heart gratitude and joy of having ongoing love in life *vs.* closing down in the pain. I am continually in motion, repeating this cycle of coming back to my center, to my heart, as opposed to letting the pain be the center. One way is life-giving and the other life-taking.

This language that I use with myself and with others has become not only words I speak, but the way I live. The energy of my heart's trust reverberates through my mouth and my actions, despite the pain that exists in my heart. In its energy, it strengthens my quality of living instead of weakening it. The words you choose are a direct link into the mindset that you have and the state of your heart. So, choosing words wisely, or even just being aware of what words you are using, is a very skillful practice.

Language as an energy and a tool is so powerful. We all should develop our capacity to use it skillfully. The ability to cultivate life-giving, life-supporting language comes from the heart. When you can speak from the voice of your heart and not from the pain voice of your hurt, that is when the power of the unified positive and negative together, can give a sense of whole life-connection. Sometimes, to reach the depth of truly hearing your own heart, it takes a multidimensional mix of language: hearing your own thoughts, feeling your own emotions, noticing your body's holding, feeling your spirit's nudges. A person must grow with their life experiences to be able to have a heart that trusts itself. But note that the heart can only learn to listen when it is open; just as you can only see if your eyes are open to seeing.

## The Light Behind Using Words Wisely

Here are a few truths to remember:

You are constantly in relationship.

Language is the connector.

Language is everywhere and in everything,

Connecting you everywhere with everything.

Language *is* Word.

Word is Energy.

Word is energy in your life.

A Bible verse comes to mind speaking of *word*, which I find so fascinating —the parallel of your words having spiritual essence in your life and "the Word" as the spiritual essence of God.

In the beginning was the Word,

and the Word was with God,

and the Word was God.

–John 1:1

God's energy through word, is the true and trustable light of your heart. The workings of God are working in you when you let them forth from the light of your heart. And when God's light in your heart pours forth it can come from you in words. Think for a moment and then write down: what are the true and trustable *words* of your heart?

God is echoing everywhere and in everything in connection with *you*. Sometimes the power in language and in word is the very energy of God shining through. That's why you must be skillful in using your words for good —to build up connection, not tear it down. It is that golden rule, I think we all have heard: do towards others what you would want done to you.

## Wholeness in Experiencing

Communication is not just words falling on ears though, it is a fully-sensorial fully-present phenomena of taking in all of the physical, emotional, mental, and spiritual cues being expressed to you simultaneously. Imagine that you are going for a job interview and are really nervous. But upon entering the interview room, you see an old friend who you have lost touch with. The moment you realize that they are going to be the one interviewing you, so much changes about how you are in that moment. Your friend greets you with a big hug, a smile, and says, "Oh my gosh, I had hoped that this was you I would be interviewing."

In this moment, you are not consciously cataloging the different dimensions that make up the wholeness of the experience of going from nervous to relaxed. Instead, all at once—you feel emotionally happy to see your friend; you mentally think, *What are the odds?*; physically your body relaxes from the nerves you had minutes ago; and spiritually you have a sense of being in the right place at the right time. The experience is fully integrated. All of these dimensions converge in a mere moment. We don't decipher this moment so fragmentedly because it is already a naturally integrated experience. However, the *vibrance* with which we can experience our integrated living can be sharpened by our awareness and our openness. And in the sometimes mixed-messaging of communication, the vibrant dimensionality can in turn keep you in-touch with receiving accurately what is happening in your life.

When a person has mental blinders on, they are less likely to pick up on subtleties. When a person can become an open observer, that's when the subtleties are able to be picked up on a little louder. How do you become an open observer? Sometimes it is just sitting still and being open. This would be the passive, yin approach. But sometimes it is initiating an open dialogue. This would be the active yang approach. Both are avenues leading to the same thing: connection.

This brings me to a question: are you open to hearing what is being communicated? When someone is open to hear, they are open to the possibility of a different perspective. When a person has a bad taste for something, how open are they to seeing it in a different light? Sometimes it seems people can attach to the bad taste and deem it absolute. But does one rotten tomato mean every tomato is rotten? Not likely. And so, one bad taste does not mean everything about a person, place, or thing is going to be rotten. And maybe your interpretation is skewed at times. It's like a parent scolding a kid. The kid receives it as, *I did wrong—do you love me still?* But the parent sends it as, *I love you and want to teach you right.* They are varying perceptions. Neither one is wrong. Things are being seen by different eyes with a different view. When you are in your own head and stuck in your own experience, you are less likely to pick up on the subtleties and deeper truths being communicated. Openness allows you clearer hearing with which to listen to these deeper truths.

## Openness and Awareness Help in Seeing Deeper Truth

On April 8th, when I got the call at 5:30 a.m. that my husband was in cardiac arrest at the hospital, I was swallowed up in the darkness of trauma and the urgency of *I have to do something*, but all I could do was pray. And pray big—like end-of-the-world prayer. End-of-*my*-world prayer. I cried so hard my eyelids crushed against each other; it felt like they were being turned inside out along their edges. The force with which they were being squeezed reflected the vice grip in my chest, tightly strangling my heart. My body started to shake uncontrollably. My teeth chattered. My mind, consumed by fear, thought, *Is he going to die? Nooooo!* My spirit wanted to cling to him. The emotional sharpness of shock, confusion, and all-consuming desperation was instant. Literally minutes later, the phone rang again and I answered it to hear, "We were able to resuscitate your husband. He is currently on a breathing tube and his heart is beating. We will know more as the day goes on and will update you." What followed was a heart-shattering, sinking feeling but also a strong hope.

Two days later, on April 10th, when we decided to let him pass on naturally without continued life support, I could have stayed totally stuck in the trauma of it all. And don't get me wrong—in many ways I still was and maybe even still am. But there was also an opening. An opening being communicated to me. Something holding my hand and encouraging me into the language of love and acceptance *vs.* the frozen fear of trauma. That day, as I drove to the hospital to see him, with our children in the back seat, quietly cuddled up with blankets for comfort, I reflected on the fact that his death day was going to be Good Friday. It was the *same day* that my mom had passed away, nineteen years before. In that poignant synchronicity, something in me knew that God had a hand in this.

Upon arriving, the feeling in the room supported a feeling of peace. I had relief—relief that I could finally be there for him and hold his hand, stroke his hair, and kiss his face. I was able to find the strength to be his strength to let go. Due to COVID-19 restrictions, we had not been allowed to visit for most of his stay. Sadly, only two of us were allowed now. But one was me, and I thank God for that—for letting me be there for him in his moment of release.

The physical feeling of him passing was beautiful. I lay there with him, on top of him actually, as I had climbed into the hospital bed with him. I needed to be close, as close as humanly possible. He needed me close. I put my arms around him and laid my head upon his chest. I could hear his heart beat and feel it thump against my ear. That is a language I will never forget, the language of his heart saying, *Goodbye, my love.* And the language of my love holding him and saying back, *I am here for you.* The subtle language of the inaudible energy communicated through the room was one of peace and of presence. I felt calm with him in that moment. I felt his peace in my heart and humility about how life had orchestrated itself to this exact moment, hearing and feeling my husband slip away into the unknown.

His mom, the only other person allowed to be there, got a prayer book out and said a little prayer. Then she began to read the Lord's Prayer. "Our Father, who art in heaven." *Tha-thunk* went his heartbeat, pulsing in my ear. "Hallowed be thy name. Thy Kingdom come." *Tha-thunk* went his heart. "Thy will be done on earth as it is in heaven." *Tha-thunk* went his heart as the beat of his life left his body.

His heart never beat again. His lungs never breathed again. The still silence of the moment I was holding onto also left the room as so much flooded in, taking its place. Yes, there is a language shared that goes much deeper than the surface—the language of that which connects us is deeper than the bone, but as surface as the smile: it is the language of life.

I think about that day and am in awe of how I wasn't frozen in fear and trauma…but I could have been. Instead, through the language breathing through me, through that moment on earth, through my husband and God, I was allowed eyes to see his death as beautiful. His death was beautiful. His dying still a tragedy. It was two sides of the same coin: the coin of life's circle being completed.

The truth of being immersed in a sea of energy is that you affect the energy at the same time that it affects you. Duality of—the inside to the out, and the outside to the in—makes up the flow of oneness and can give you a connected sense of wholeness. Your sense of oneness with what *is*, sometimes despite what is, connects you to wholeness because you are not separate but a part of all that you experience. And at the same time, you are *how* you experience it. I *was* that very moment; I embodied it embodying me. My internal and external language was in flowing connection. The degree of the sense of wholeness or oneness that you have is based off of how open you are to receiving and giving in life's flow—not bracing against life, in its challenges, but embracing it despite them. Perhaps there is an openness to speak up louder for what has before been left unsaid, to fill in between the lines, letting the language of life become clearer in yourself and to the world. If you feel disconnected in life, then how you are in life is not working for you, and you need to be brave and willing to assess and adjust this. Sometimes, how you are is the biggest truth. Sometimes, it's a truth you'd rather not keep the same— and that's where you ask for help. And where can help come from? Help comes through relationship.

# 3

# FROM DARKNESS TO LIGHT

## *Your Relationship With Yourself*

One morning in October 2020, my nine-year-old daughter, Marin, was sitting on a stool at our kitchen island going on about something as I stood over a pan of ham-and-cheese scrambled eggs. I knew she was talking to me, but I was spaced out and didn't really hear what she was saying.

"Mom, are you listening?" she asked in frustration.

Just then, my thirteen-year-old son, Gavin, came in and sat down. Never missing a moment to say, "Shut-up, Marin," the two of them were off as if a gunshot had announced the start of their arguing match. All of a sudden, anger, frustration, distress, and defeat took...me...over. With intensity and muscle, I raised up that flat black spatula with egg and cheese stuck to it and started to beat it down on the edge of our kitchen stove.

"I can't take it. You guys fighting all the time." I shouted.

Their banter stopped in stunned response to me, their mom, cracking like the fragile egg shells on the counter. The eggs were done, and so was I. As I continued to have my tantrum, I repeatedly slammed down the spatula, feeling rage arising from within and exerting itself out. As my body tired from the burst, I stopped what I was doing—immediately recognizing: *that was not good.*

I turned with pan and spatula in hand and scooped out the eggs onto their plates. My anger still fresh in my voice, I said, "That was really bad behavior on my part. But I am at my limit right now. Just don't talk at all because I can't take anything else landing on me right now."

A short aftershock followed of Marin yelling at me and Gavin yelling at her. Then they both settled in to eating their eggs in silence as I stomped around the kitchen, letting my temper sizzle down like the pan in the sink. Shortly after, I recovered. I could speak more easily, and was open to receiving my kids' comments.

"Oh my gosh, Mom, you were crazy."

"I know," I sighed.

My kids had been home from school after the death of their father fell over us and COVID-19 fell over the world. We were in one of the fortunate school districts that had resumed at the start of September 2020; yet a month in, it felt like we were still finding our new groove with the dramatic changes that had taken over our old life. I felt like I was moving along as best as I could, continuing to find my way without Corey. I had closed down my business seeing clients as an AcuEnergetics® practitioner, started writing this book, and had just been accepted into a program to earn a degree as a dental assistant. This all was a little scary and unnerving. On top of it, with the busy flow of single-parent life, I started to slack off with the self-care I desperately needed. I was able to do weekly healthful activities but not daily. I could feel this lack compounding most obviously on the days when I did clear space in my agenda to sit and meditate. My mind and body would quiet with feeling my breath—but under the surface something more was bubbling. Through the opening awareness in my meditation, I would start to experience the uncovering of a deep, inner tremble. I could feel the shaky quiver throughout my body, like a wobbly wheel ready to fall off. The quieter I got, the more that my inner unstableness grew louder to me and I realized: *this is how I am all of the time.* Under the surface, shaky, while on the surface, living over my own unsteadiness as best as I could.

Continuing to lack self-care, the pressure had built. And on the morning of the egg incident, I found out that I was not fighting off the mounting angst well enough. I *thought* I had been managing it by decompressing it here and there. In hindsight, I see that it needed to spill over so that I could be jolted into recognizing I was carrying too much fear, anger, and sadness, just ready to burst at the seams.

## The Light of Seeing the Dark Self

That morning, along with breakfast, I served up both awareness and honesty in being an observer of my own bad behavior. I later called a friend to dish on my insanity and laugh about what a lunatic I probably looked like. Then I started to think about how I owed myself some gratitude and compassion. I now knew that I needed to get more in touch with what was really bothering me: my darker feelings, that trembling fear and anger under the surface. The inner rage that I had little idea had been festering so powerfully within me was saying, *Hello, do you see me now?* In a big way. And I heard it because I was listening. I did not shelter, sugar-coat, or divert blame. I saw myself in my own error and accepted it so that I could work with it— work with myself in connection. Like a rubber band stretched too thin, I snapped—not just from the situation at hand, but from so much more. Including not finding ways to navigate my stress. In this moment, it was my behavior that needed some repair. I was honest in admitting that to myself. I can even say I was quick in admitting it because, as I was still hitting the spatula on the stove, I knew what I was doing was *cray-cray*, as we say in our house.

After I had taken space to calm down, I was able to talk about it openly. Honesty and openness are growth-supporting. If I had had my tantrum and then turned around and blamed it solely on my kids fighting, I would have been so far from being in touch with the real truth of the situation. I have learned that when you have struggle in your life, it can be transformational; only you get to decide how it transforms you—for better or for worse. In this moment, I understood that my bad behavior could be used as a launching point to choose transformation for the better.

## Time for Insight

Pause now, get out your journal, and give yourself a chance to reflect on how you behave in conflict. Ask yourself:

- *Is it easy to see and accept the part I play in heightened situations?*
- *Do I have awareness around how I am during conflict and use it to repair and grow?*
- *Is someone else always to blame for my issues?*
- *Who takes ultimate responsibility?*
- *Who should take responsibility?*

You have the ultimate say in how your life is. Take another moment to think about something specific that is bothering you and explore how you are a part of the issue.

## Growth in Self-Honesty

If you are compelled to lay blame, you must also be willing to look at what you did or didn't do that might have added to the situation. Taking responsibility is a sign of maturity and openness. You must look at your self-conduct in navigating a remedy for issues in your life. Remember that old saying, "Honesty is the best medicine"? It's a saying for a reason; there is truth in it. Be honest with yourself. Self-honesty is the number one value to uphold in your relationship with yourself. It can even be said that it is the first step in self-connection. If you deceive yourself, then nothing and nobody can help you because you can't be reached.

Your relationship with yourself *seems* like it should be the clearest and most direct relationship you have. It appears there is zero gap when it comes to the connection of you to yourself. But it is actually a relationship that can be quite distant. It can even be your most dysfunctional relationship. And its dysfunction bleeds out into all other relationships that you have. This is why you need to explore your self-relationship first. After all, *you* are front and center in your connection with all other relationships because you are *who* you experience all relationships through. It is valuable to spend time with yourself to understand, develop, and nurture self-connection. The self is the only path to connection on any level. It is the way in which you bring yourself back to who you are in the truth of God's light that you carry.

As you get into exploring your self-connection, my hope is that you nurture it by giving yourself grace, because no one is perfect. In God's eyes, no one stands above or below you. We are each in our own place with our own host of blessings and shortcomings. Maybe you can learn to embrace both within yourself. True connection is not selective, seeing only the good and ignoring the bad. That is sheltering delusion—no matter how falsely superior it might make you feel. True connection is also not selective in seeing the bad and ignoring the good. That too is delusion, one that traps you in a personal sense of inferiority. Self-connection is neither about being superior or inferior; it is about being real. Can you be real with yourself? True connection to the self allows the wisdom of seeing both good and bad and ignoring neither. It is open and purposeful in knowing and navigating your own personal duality.

## Disconnection from Yourself

Even though you are with yourself twenty-four seven, 365 days out of the year, there is still room for disconnect. When disconnect is present in your primary relationship—with yourself—and you believe your own lies of superiority or inferiority, a whole host of issues can ripple out, like waves crashing over you and others in your life. Disconnection to yourself boils down to the presence of self-deceit. Honesty is the foundational piece you must establish within yourself to re-establish connection.

You can start to open up this relationship right now by being open to look at what's under your surface. Be bravely honest, and answer this question for your own good: *in what ways am I deceiving myself?* Write your thoughts down.

As painful or scary as your answer might be, it is healing. Sometimes, to heal properly, a wound needs to be unwrapped and exposed to the open air. Just as your body needs oxygen to heal, your pain needs breathing room to feel it, in order to heal it. You can't hold your breath against your internal wounds forever and expect them to just be okay. That is deception through ignoring. That is when tensions accumulate and you become like the rubber band, snapping in unconscious ways. It might cover up and make things appear okay from the outside, but the wound still festers without giving it air.

Some general deceptions may sound like:

- I don't need any help.
- I can't do this on my own.
- When I get a new _____, then I will be better.
- It will blow over on its own.
- I'm not good enough to advance in my career.
- I'm above dealing with ignorant people.
- That doesn't bother me anymore.
- I will never get through this loss.

There are many others. Hopefully, you have started to see an underlying deception of your own. Honesty always makes a situation more workable and empowers you in knowing your own truth. In lies and deceit, the possibility to rectify something is cut off.

## Connecting through You

Not everything about yourself is easy to see or feel. When there is something in your life that seems reasonable to be experiencing emotionally, in regards to a circumstance, and you are *not* experiencing it, be aware. There are layers to healing, so as you move through giving self-attention and self-nurturing, it can be normal for latent feelings and thoughts to surface. Sometimes unacknowledged thoughts and feelings are stored deep inside.

Anger is a normal part of grief and is one of the five stages of grief identified by psychiatrist Elisabeth Kübler-Ross. That fact didn't matter to me. I didn't feel like I needed to fit into anyone else's box of what grieving was after my mom passed away when I was twenty-one. I had previously learned about these stages in my studies as an undergraduate psychology major, but I didn't give them much thought. I was just living my personal experience.

It wasn't until years later in my thirties, while lying on a healing table receiving energy therapy and processing through emotional blocks, that my anger was accessed. I finally felt angry about not having my mom in my life. I was angry that she died so young, at age 52. I was angry that both she and I missed out on so much since her death. Like, *super pissed*. I told the woman facilitating the healing session that I felt like I needed to move my body. The anger was coming up in me with so much force it had to have a physical outlet. I wasn't going to yell because we were in a public building, so I let my body be my expressive release. My arms and legs thrashed and my fists and heels came banging down on the table. Inside, I was screaming, *Nooooo*. It was an intense moment, but naturally its intensity did not last. The intensity was a doorway for me to see, feel, and understand that I *do* have anger about my mom's early death, for her painful death, and for her absence. I felt surprisingly whole in that moment. Going into the session that day, I did not know I was going to go there, but it was time. I was ready to finally see and feel that part of myself that I had closed to.

I have recently experienced a latent emotion rear its head in continuing to process the layers of grief surrounding Corey's death, too. In this case, anger has not been a problem; I have felt that emotion right from the start. But resentment had been foreign to me. In fact, in being so in touch with myself and aware of what I was feeling and what I was not feeling, I had actually wondered if I was unconsciously blocking my resentment. Sometimes I would think, *Shouldn't I feel resentment towards being here alone, towards having our dreams crushed, and having to rebuild without him?* Even though the thoughts made sense in my mind, I was not *feeling* resentment within myself. Then, one day, a perfect storm of things shifted me and the resentment within was able to bubble up and finally be felt.

It was my second birthday without Corey, about a year and a half after he had passed. That morning our son was ill and needed to be taken into the doctor. I also had a college class to get to, and our daughter needed help getting ready for school. Later that day, she had a cross country meet as well. In quickly working out how to manage all of this, I decided I needed to ditch my daughter and leave her to fend for herself in getting ready and arranged for her to get a ride to school with the neighbor. Part of this decision was that I needed to get my son into the clinic before they opened so that he would be guaranteed to be the first patient seen at 7:30 a.m. so that I could get him back home to give myself just enough time to get to campus for my class. I had a total of three classes that day, so I knew I would also be ditching my son and that he would have to be home alone, sick, and taking care of himself all day. In taking him in so early to the doctor, I was avoiding having to take him later after my classes, so that I could then attend my daughter's cross country meet and be there to cheer her on. We weren't going to be getting home until 6:00 p.m. when the normal nightly routine would dominate: dinner, homework, showers, and bedtime. And all of this on my birthday! *Ah,* there was *resentment.* I could feel it for real for the first time since Corey's passing. The capacity had been in me all along, but for whatever reason it just wasn't being brought out in me. But now I could feel: *this is what resentment feels like.* I suffered through that day, angry and cold. I avoided feeling any joy in it being my birthday. I said a flat "thanks" to the *"happy birthdays"* when appropriate, all the while resenting that I didn't have my partner to share the joys and the challenges with.

I suspect that everyone has at times experienced being at odds with herself or himself. I was at odds with feeling anger about my mom's death. I was at odds with feeling resentment about being a single parent in the wake of my husband's death. When you are at odds with yourself, there is a distance between how you are and how you really feel. In this distance you can do things you don't really mean; sometimes you make mistakes;

sometimes you mistakenly hurt others. Sometimes, causing others to hurt stems from your own hurting inadvertently.

This is why your foundation must be an honest self-relationship. When you can be honest with yourself first in self-relationship, then that is when you can start to reach out to other relationships for self-support. When at odds with oneself, there is a need to connect with God to surrender and find a clearer way through. There is a need to connect with others to gain supportive perspective and resources. And there is a need to connect with the earth to get physical supports—nourishment, space, and healing aesthetics. It took the outside support of an energy therapist in one case and the outside aligning of circumstances beyond my control in the other, for me to get in touch with what was a hidden layer of experiencing the wholeness of my life.

You can't do it all by yourself. You aren't designed to do it all by yourself. No one is. And neither is the environment we live in as a whole designed for us to do it all by ourself. People live in symbiosis, one affecting the other. So, nope, you're not meant to do it alone, ever—hence your natural inclination for relationship and connection. Don't cut yourself off at the foot by thinking that relationship and connection is not important for you in *any* of the four relationships; connection is what you are *made of* and it is what you are *made for.*

Even though you are not meant to do it alone, the flip-side of the coin of life tells you that *no one can do it for you, you must do it for yourself.* But it is *both-and* at the same time. The two dualities together show the bigger union of oneness in working relationship. There is both inner work and outer work to helping yourself. You must be your own best friend and, in doing so, seek the supports to help you get through. But if you are not first connected to yourself, this makes reaching for the external support much harder because disconnection with yourself breeds disconnection with everything else. So, prioritize your ability to connect with *you.*

Connecting with yourself can have its own complexity as a relationship. In wholeness, there is unity: you are one whole being put together from many parts. You also have duality: two sides of yourself in opposing nature. Examples of this across different dimensions are: physically, you need activity and rest; emotionally, you have good and bad moods; mentally, you have positive and negative thoughts; and spiritually, you can be open or closed.

Yet you also have multidimensionality—the blending together of those varying parts and dimensions. Complexity is complicated, so it is not surprising that sometimes you are none too clear for even yourself to understand. However, when you aren't clear, that breeds a bigger gap of disconnect, which allows subsequent issues to fester and boil. Your self-relationship can either have a vast divide like the Grand Canyon or the warmth of closeness like skin-to-skin. Ask yourself right now: *which direction am I moving in when it comes to my relationship with myself? Am I moving closer to myself? Or have I been driving in a bigger wedge, pushing myself away?*

## The Body's Holistic Connection

Self-awareness can come through practicing hearing your own thoughts, watching your behaviors, and feeling your emotions. But it can also come through your body connection, as the body is a very real dimension of your wholeness. The body is not separate from mind, emotion, or spirit. They all are integrated. Your emotional and mental buildup is also a buildup in the body. My life and grief coach, Ima Morrisitte, once said to me, "We don't feel big emotions without there being a physical side effect." The same idea is supported in the work of Bessel van der Kolk in *The Body Keeps the Score: Brain, Mind, and Body in the Healing of Trauma*, in which he talks about going from the "bottom up," as he calls it, or from body to mind, by healing traumas through physical feeling experiences that support neural rewiring of stress responses.

Depression is a good example of the body's capacity to hold mental and emotional energy that affects the physical self. Depression is a mood disorder that also affects the physical body in disrupting sleep, appetite, and energy level. But it has even been linked to physical pain such as headaches or body aches and gastrointestinal issues. Depression moving from mind into body is one directional flow of this condition—tending to wind things up. But the other direction of it moving from body to mind actually holds a potential to supportively unwind it. In fact, many scientific studies have shown depression can be positively impacted by exercise. The studies show that when depressed people exercise, they feel less depressed. A *Psychology Today* article reviewed the summation of twenty-five such studies, confirming that, "Regardless of individual predisposition… moderate exercise not only treats, but can prevent depression." In exercise, there is physical movement of stagnant physical energy, at the same time as there is production of positive body chemistry in the release of endorphins. Bottom line: body tissue holds your baggage, and the holding affects how you are in your body, mind, emotion, and spiritual self.

One day, while getting a deep-tissue massage, the masseuse was working the muscles of my shoulders and neck where all of my stress tends to structurally bind-up. I couldn't help but tense against the pressure applied to my stress points as he attempted to work them out. I petitioned against the intense pressure; but in his skillful craft, he knew what was needed and eased me into the process instead of dulling the therapy down. He instructed me to do the movement myself to work out the kink as he held the spot with applied pressure. As I moved my arm around freely, the pain intensity in the kink grew and then dispersed. My movement under the pressure was causing release. Still, it was not an easy progression—moving from one lump of bound up tissue to another.

"Ouch," I couldn't help but say out loud as the pain unsilenced from within my muscles and came out through my lips. My hands were the most shockingly painful. I didn't know I could hold so much tension in my boney, little hands. He dug into the muscle, gliding his fingers until stopping at a knot, making me *stay with feeling the pain*, until it finally opened up, and was allowed to soften, supporting smoothness and ease.

"Like butter," the masseuse said.

Sitting in pain is uncomfortable, but pain is there for a reason. It needs attention, and working with, so that it too can have release. For the rest of the massage, I was able to watch the cycle of pain in my body as it would heighten and then dissipate. With each new knot discovered, I was brought back into physically experiencing deep pain. I allowed myself to feel it, not stop it, noticing that by giving the pain time with therapeutic pressure and presence, the pain naturally began to dissipate. This was an enlightening experience, linking awareness that sometimes it too is necessary to therapeutically massage our emotional holdings like we can our physical ones, because the same dynamic is at play here—a means to some relief and improvement.

## Working with Your Pain

When you have inner pressure and it gets pushed on, release is inevitable; but when you *constructively and actively* push on it, its release is more therapeutic because you are in connection with the process of it being pushed and pulled on for the release. This is why therapy is therapeutic. It is consciously applied attention for the purpose of relief. Whether it be physical, spiritual, emotional, or mental, its application holds potential for your betterment. So, own the pain you feel. Own the pain you've caused. Notice it, work to understand it, and give space in the process to see what could be in wholeness of allowing the good and the bad to be as one within you, in conscious awareness.

Pain so often creates that monumental divide you don't want to look at, work through, or touch with a ten-foot pole. *Oh, that's just the past,* you may tell yourself. *I already worked through that.* But pain gets carried along even if you don't know it is traveling with you. And it can make its home deep within your tissues and cells. When it's loud in the body, it points out that you need to give yourself some attention. And sometimes it gets louder until you can't not give it attention. Sometimes problems get worse before they get better. We each have to face ourselves and be brave in working through the knots, whatever dimension they are stemming from, for them to have the opportunity to get better and let you get better.

You know what is so meaningful about someone saying, "I am sorry?" It's that they are aware of the pain that they've caused. It's validating and healing. So never be afraid to apologize to someone. But also know that seeing your own pain and being with your pain is like saying to yourself, *I am sorry for myself that I hurt,* and it has the same effect of validation and healing.

Turning away from your pain just stunts its process of integration, keeping it from its natural place of being an actualized part of yourself. However, be aware that there is a balance needed here between the opposite ends of never feeling your pain and feeling it all the time. While it is not helpful to ignore it, it also is not helpful to live in it all of the time. Your pain is a part of you, but it is not you. Your fullness of experiencing you goes beyond experiencing your pain. That said, seeing and feeling your pain, along with being honest with yourself, are both worthy of your time and attention. Being open to see the good and the bad can give you the eyes to see a deeper truth. Insight is the elixir of enlightenment.

## Allowing the Opening of Yourself

In the experience of developing your openness and awareness, you get fresh eyes with which to see your life. The more open your eyes are to see, the more the light can come in. This light of awareness is then able to shine on the darker, shaded corners within yourself. In the spaces where warm, life-giving, golden rays are needed for growth and maturing. As Hafiz said about the blossoming rose, "the encouragement of light against its being" allowed it to "open its heart and give to this world all of its beauty." You are even more beautiful and magnificent than the rose. So, won't you also allow yourself to feel light against your heart so that you may open to your own beauty?

Through the practice of cultivating open ears to listen inwardly and having honesty with yourself about what those ears hear, you too are emitting more light of inner truth into your being. The two light sources of outer and inner, nourish you in such a way as to create the proper soil for a new way of being to take root and grow. Bringing goodness to your heart—goodness you feel for yourself. Imagine that as you grow within, you grow closer to yourself in your heart—closer to feeling your connected wholeness.

The lamp of the body is the eye.

If therefore your eye is good, your whole body will be full of light.

But if your eye is bad, your whole body will be full of darkness.

If therefore the light that is in you is darkness, how great is that darkness.

—Matthew 6:22–23

The eye of perception colors the space that the light shines into. That space is you. Do you feel that you see life with a lens of dimness? Do you feel you have an inner mechanism that causes you to turn towards where there is light in the world? If sometimes you get deep and dark within yourself, you must know you are just like the rose. You need only to be moved to a place with more light to take in more light. You always have the capacity to shift towards the light. The light is always there for you to turn to.

## Identity in Crisis

When I was a teenager, I struggled with myself. Gosh, don't most of us in those awkward years? It started around age thirteen; something inside me came crashing down, and I felt alone and deeply at odds with who I was. There wasn't anything specific that happened to set me off in such a dramatic way, I was just growing up and not exempt from growing pains. I was going through a massive amount of hormonal and body changes while also trying to figure out my own identity through the cloudiness of teenage confusion. In fact, in my memory of that dark time, I would say that I loathed myself. Yet, in the light of today, I see there was no need to feel so hateful.

Still, at the time, I was hurting and hurting myself through a lack of self-care. On many occasions, I remember sitting on the bathroom counter, feet in the empty sink, so that I could get close to the mirror. I would pick at my face, critique the way I looked, and stress about all of the zits that kept popping up, day after day. I felt disgusted by myself. I had a really high inner cringe factor. We only had one bathroom, so eventually someone would knock on the door. I would exit with a scowl, wearing the way I felt on my face. Not wanting to talk to anyone, I would then shut myself in my room and turn on the radio to drown out the noise in my world and, if I was lucky, the noise in my head. Often, my thoughts would ramble about how pitiful and embarrassing I was. It's a wonder the nasty things that one can say to oneself. Isolated and feeding my own mind garbage, I believed I was the unlovable loser that I felt like.

I wasn't in touch with believing that others cared about me either. I was in complete disillusionment; I had a really good family, good-hearted parents George and Diane, and caring siblings Lynnette, Aaron, and Ryan, who all loved each other. Yet I was darkened by inner loneliness despite this outer world of light. I did not treat myself with care or compassion because I didn't care about myself. When you don't care about yourself, it completely sours your whole experience of the world. It sours how you behave towards yourself and how you are in relationship with others. So, not only was I closed off to myself, I was closed off to those who cared for me. I had a dark perspective towards who I was, how I looked, where I fit, and it took me under. I held myself captive in the disillusioned darkness. I was stuck in a cyclical reoccurring pattern that felt like it had a death grip on my life and was squeezing the light out of me. It was a swirling, drowning, pattern of aloneness, self-hate, and morbid thinking. And again, when pain and tension build, they need a release. For me, at that time, it was writing poetry.

In my self-isolation, confusion, and disconnection, the light of self-awareness was still able to shine through in words. My writing allowed me to reflect how I felt back to myself so that I could see and witness myself. This preserved a small sliver of self-connection to hold onto. This is a poem that I wrote at the disillusioned age of thirteen.

"Tearful Plea"

This hateful feeling you have inside,

It comes on strong and you have to hide,

It grows and grows,

But still no one knows.

I'm losing faith,

I'm opening the gate,

I'm almost there,

But who gives a care.

Little by little,

The blood starts to trickle,

And then pour,

And soon I will be nothing more . . .

Then a body six feet under,

Then a soul lost in thunder,

A fading memory,

And the nightmares of my tearful plea.


Sometimes, the choking off from the light was self-induced in the strange swirl of change, emotion, and emptiness. I couldn't see a way out of it and at the same time I was making it worse for myself, stuck in the swirling of it all. That's how life catches you when you get stuck in repeating a pattern that keeps you down. You acclimate to it and get used to its round-and-round repetition. Each time it knocks you down, you recover—but only for the next crashing wave to come around and *pow*—knock you down again.

And yet, even though I was in a space of feeling stuck I had movement in my words. My words were dark and my perspective negative, but it felt good to express myself and be creative. A part of me warmed up to liking this part of myself that could create through self-expression as I found that I actually liked pieces of what I could create in writing. Maybe honesty and artistry together are perfection, because there was definitely perfection in combining the two to give my soul what it was needing.

I had a friend, Kathleen, who also wrote poems and, on occasion, I would open up to her and share something that I had written. We would sit in her room; she on her bed and me on the floor, leaning up against the wall, and we would write. The openness felt safe in that it was reciprocated; she too would share her poems with me.

"Your words are so beautiful," I would tell her.

And she would also compliment me, "Wow, this is really good."

Sharing what I had written gave me something to feel proud of. It put me in the experience of seeing that someone else liked something about me. I could put words to paper and found meaning in doing so.

## The Power of Acknowledging How You Feel

I didn't know then that in my teenage writing I was actively connecting with myself, but nonetheless it was helpful. I think that's why journaling can be so therapeutic for people because it naturally puts you in touch with yourself. When stuck in that spiraling pattern of the uncomfortable area of life you are living in, you have to first recognize that *where you are* is stuck and spinning. Bring consciousness to the unconscious. It is like a record player with a skipping record; it keeps playing the same lyric over and over and over until you come in and *shift up and out* of the repeating. When you shift up and out with awareness and action, your potential to get unstuck is opened up. Sometimes, the very thing that can awaken you to your stuck-ness is letting yourself notice how you feel and then acknowledging that the pattern repeating does not feel in alignment with what you want. Through having openness to how you feel, you are given insight for becoming aware of the steps you need to take. The effort and attention needed for re-alignment are revealed.

When things in your life become too engrained as a pattern, you can grow unconscious in them. Think about driving home; you know every turn and every road to take because it is such an engrained pattern. So, when you are preoccupied with something else during the drive it is easy to check-out and be on autopilot just going through the motions. You arrive home, but can't quite remember taking the last two turns because you were not conscious in the actions you were taking. Instead, you were operating through a program for what you were doing.

This could play out just as easily in a different area of life, like just getting by at work instead of reaching for where you can excel. Programmed behavior could also show up in parent style: handling conflict resolution by just giving in to the whining child. Or in feeling dissatisfied with one's health, yet always indulging in a big, greasy breakfast. A cyclical nature could also be avoiding the pain points in your life because you keep telling yourself you don't have the time, energy, or the means to deal with them. And pain, in general, can be very disillusioning and exhausting, causing you to unconsciously numb even more deeply. Thus, the cycle repeats under the surface without you keying-in that—there it is, running in the background of your life.

## Time for Insight

Do you have any areas of your life where you are unconsciously driving on auto-pilot? It's time look deeper, because how can you ever get out of it if you don't first *see* you have something to get out of? Take a moment to look at *what jumps out to you as a pattern in your life*. Write it down in your journal.

Now think about something that seems to be happening a lot in your life. Write it down. Maybe there is a conversation you are having, over and over? Write it down. Perhaps things being left unsaid? Write it down. Is there something you keep circling around? A pattern you keep repeating in behavior, mental attitude, emotional instability, or relational turmoil? Are there actions that keep coming up that don't feel in alignment with what you would hope for in your life? Write down all of your impressions, no matter how solid or slight they may be.

Now look back at your list and ask yourself: *could it be that I am not fully conscious about where I am driving too?* For each scenario, answer for yourself as clearly as possible: *where do I want to head in this area?* This will help you create a road map of reconnection for yourself, highlighting how you might begin moving from unconsciousness to consciousness.

You have been doing an amazing job taking the time to stop and answer some of the questions I have been asking, but it can be equally insightful to just open to a blank page and write down how you are feeling. Journaling is therapeutic and enlightening because what comes forth is an unmasking of what's under the surface. And when the mask comes off, not only can you see better, but you can better be seen. I encourage you to give it a go. So, open a fresh page in your journal and open *yourself* to the blank page. It will be a good listener, never judgmental, and will always have space for what you have to say. There are no rules. There is only open expression and, in openness, sometimes understanding is allowed as parts of yourself that are otherwise quiet and stored away are given a wide-open blank page *to exist.*

## Light Source as Connection

As a teenage girl, even in my darkness, I was still allowed glimmers of myself that were *maybe* worth resurrecting. Despite my angst, there was something that kept catching the light and shining. Something that felt worthwhile. I often disconnected from my family, friends, and myself, but interestingly that was a time when I felt closely connected to nature. I was deeply lacking in three out of the four relationships, but my relationship with the earth kept showing up to carry me through. There were always sources of light shining towards me, but where I saw the light reaching out best was through the gentle, heart-touching beauty of the earth.

When all strong bonds of relationship appeared to be in critical condition, this one relationship presented itself more strongly, giving me something to feel connected to. Eventually, through my awed connection with the earth, came whispers of my growing connection to God, as well. I found that God felt synonymous with the natural world. Nature was my place to connect and feel soothed by an innate connection to vibrant life. The light of it reached out and filled me up—through the moon and the stars, the feel of the breeze, the light of a candle, the sound of the wave, the dance of the tree. Earth was my illuminating source.

Time went on and light began to shine *out* from me through my feeling my connection to nature and God, and then finally through greater connection to a few close friends. And all of that light I was starting to put out eventually circled back around to me. I started to feel more connected to myself as my glimmer of hope for self-understanding also became stronger— again through written words. When I wrote poetry during this period, the words would just flow out from me, and then I'd read them and something in me would be reflected back; I'd have a deeper understanding about how I was feeling.

As an inexperienced teenager, I could not recognize that my struggle was short-term. I was purely in the mix and in the emotion of it all. Because of this unconsciousness, I didn't know how to ask for the connections that I needed. I was stuck in the tight, dark enclosure of metamorphosis, in the disharmony of my inner and outer worlds, changing from child to grown-up.

All of us have been there—having parts of ourselves that are immature, even childish, and that have strides to make in waking up and growing up. It is not an experience unique to me. It is not even an experience unique to being young, because it certainly is something that can happen as an adult, too. Just because a person has biologically grown up does not mean they have left their childish mentality, emotions, or behavior behind. Growing up does not mean you have reached you maximum maturity. You keep growing … *if* you are lucky.

Fortunate for humanity, we have a natural inclination toward growth. You are physically and spiritually built to grow, to age, and mature. Unfortunately, struggle is a natural side effect of growth. Disharmony is sometimes the natural growing pain of going through metamorphosis and developing into the person you are meant to become. Even today, you are not done growing and changing. Being in an uncomfortable place can inspire us to wiggle our way out to find a new day and a new way. To grow wings and to take flight. The language of the butterfly is synonymous with this growth, but plants have this language, too. A plant that takes root buried between rocks weaves its way around the rocks until it gets a better position in the light. So, too, it is okay to grow and become a different version of who you are to be more in contact with greater light for yourself.

Connecting with your consciousness, your self-awareness is the light that illuminates the path and lets you see which direction you are heading in. This light of awareness not only casts sight upon the path to take but will illuminate those hard shadows that need a good looking into as well. Turn towards the light, and feel the light within and around you because, like a plant, humans too need light to grow.

The light sources are your supportive relationships that lift you up, not drag you down into the dark. The light can come from God, from others, and from connectivity to the healing of Mother Earth. And yes, the light can come from inside yourself, as you are never separate from the light that has been your source for all of time. Can you identify your light sources and list them? The people and things that energize you with warmth and goodness and lift you up.

## Growth from Light Leaves an Imprint on Life

Things change. Life changed. I changed. And my growth was illustrated through my words. This is a poem that I wrote at age nineteen, the tail end of coming out of my pained cocoon of teenage metamorphosis.

"Eternity Will Forget"

There's a passion in the tender arch of my foot

as I walk the beaches of this earth,

Sand giving way to cushion my soul, every new inch giving birth,

While momentary indentions of the steps that follow behind me,

Are washed over untimely by the roaring mother sea.

Stopping for a moment, to glance back at the path I've made,

Having traveled so far, can no longer grasp where my soul first laid,

Lying ahead of me, is the untouched sand of time,

So, I continue on hoping to leave a mark, distinguishably mine.

If only my foot was bigger, if only my weight was more,

Then could my impression remain across this blatant shore,

But how does one beckon the sea to spare a small print of a soul,

Knowing not even the breath she brings is altered by human control.


What these words reflect to me is that I was able to move from a place of despair to a place of hope. I had completely changed my direction in life, not only towards a brighter way of being, but towards a brighter future. These words flowed through me many years ago, but I can still connect with them today. Perhaps there is meaning that speaks to you, too? Because, not only do you want to *exist*, you want to *matter*. Deep down, we all want to matter. Yet, could it be true that people are both so big and so small at the same time? Could it be that people *do* and *don't* matter at the same time, as well?

Here is duality again: you are big, but you are small. When things are intense and you feel yourself in a heavy, negative way, you can be consumed by it and it *is* big. But does this bigness in heightened feelings really matter forever, or is it just a moment? A drop of water in a bucket? When you turn the coin over from your bigness to your smallness and allow yourself to be in awe of the earth in all her majesty, and in the divinely orchestrated moments that fill in your life, you see how you are so small, and can be comforted and humbled in this awe. No matter what your current state is, being consumed by life's issues or in awe of the wide-open world full of possibility, you are right where you need to be. You might just need a little help with your perspective of where it is you are going. Are you on your way up or are you still spiraling round and round?

## Time for Insight

You are the greatest force in your life to make change for yourself. This is why you have to help yourself. But like I mentioned earlier, at the same time that light sets us up for growth, it also illuminates the shadows. It is time to shine your light of awareness on your pain, so that you may see better the part that it plays in your life. It can take bravery to start to trust in life again and let go of the pain you hold onto. Answering these questions will allow you to see your relationship with your pain. I am not sure there are any human beings without trauma and pain, so this is a condition we all share. But how each person *is* in their relationship to pain varies. Even different types of pain in a person's life can have very different ways of being handled by them.

Ask yourself these questions:

o   *What have been some of the traumas or painful moments I have suffered in life?*

o   *How did I handle them when they happened?*

o   *How do I handle them today?*

o   *Is my relationship with pain something that holds me back? What does it hold me back from?*

o   *Have I been able to find an angle of looking through my pain that lifts me up? In what way?*

o   *If not, might it be possible to make purposeful use of my pain? Can I lift myself up, despite it all?*

Often people who have big hurts can find meaning in their pain by helping others in similar situations—by taking a sad story and letting a rose grow out of it, letting some love be spared and shared, instead of destroyed. You could not be who you are today without having gone through what you have in your life. It sounds cliché, but it is absolute truth—your truth. You have both the power to help or hinder yourself. To be your own toxin that keeps you sick in body, mind, emotion, and spirit or be your medicine that aids in your healing. The potential for either is there in you. You are both sides of the coin; you are the coin. Which side do you want to lead by? Growing towards the light or being stunted?

## Expanding Light in Intuitive Consciousness

As time went on and I kept growing up and discovering myself, the weight of my dark feelings subsided. The light kept presenting itself to me, encouraging me to open and then . . . so did love, encourage me to open. Openness then became easy, as love brings a lot of light into our hearts. Over the years of feeling love and its steadiness in connection, I was able to develop a beautiful foundation of trust, including self-trust. I even felt naturalness to trust some of my own inner nudges. This set me up for later in life when the formal opportunity was presented to learn about intuition at Intuition Thursday classes; I was open and ready.

Step one of moving from darkness to light in seeking self-connection is learning to trust yourself in honest connection. Step two is letting that self-trust give you more guided direction through using your inner compass: your intuition. Having self-trust and intuition is a back-and-forth language. Trusting to check in with yourself in how you are doing while simultaneously intuiting where you are going in life. When you can be real with yourself, then you have established real connection. That real connection then becomes an inner light that illuminates your intuitive path. This intuitive connection can then double-back and add to your sense of self-trust and self-connection even more, bringing inner peace in trusting yourself, and your life, amidst its ups and downs.

The thing I was first taught about intuition through my studies was that it is an inner compass that is connected to God's light in you. And that intuition is a God-given, inner-navigation system that can guide you simply by you being in connection with yourself. But what I discovered for myself, was that I had already been using it in my life. You probably have already been using it too—maybe without even realizing it because it is a natural navigation system that is always there, whether you turn towards it or not. Think of the example of "mother's intuition" which is widely accepted as the gift of being able to pick-up on things for one's own child regarding their well-being. So too, the general gift of intuition also covers being able to pick-up on things about you, for your own good.

## The Value in Using Intuition

Only twenty minutes from our family camper, I pulled off the road into a gas station to put the top up on our red convertible Mustang. Bucky, our mini-boxer, and Marin were buckled up in the backseat, and Gavin sat beside me in the front. We had headed north midday, with plans for Corey to join us after he finished work. We had been on the road for forty minutes, and I had been watching the gray clouds for some time, trying to gauge if I needed to put the top up to avoid rain. The sky had gotten just a little darker, so I decided to not take the chance of getting dumped on, and pulled off the road to cover us.

A minute later we were back on the road continuing north. Ten more minutes down the road, I started to drive a little faster. I was hoping to get to our camper and inside before the storm started. We were almost there. There were flashes of lightning in the clouds to the northwest, and it looked like the sky could open up at any minute with rain. I had just turned down the last straight stretch of road, about three minutes from our camper, when I was suddenly hit with the feeling to *stop*. Instead of accelerating, I took my foot off the gas and pressed down on the brake to slow us down so that I could pause to connect with this sudden feeling. I got a sinking feeling in my stomach, and a thought ran through my head, *I should turn around.*

"What are you doing, Mom?" Gavin asked.

"Hang-on, buddy. I am feeling like maybe we shouldn't be here so I am just trying to decide what to do," I told him as I made a full stop in the middle of the road. My logical mind popped in and I thought about how the camper was just a hop, skip, and a jump away and that we could get there and get inside. But the energy in my body felt like I had come into contact with a wall—like if I tried to drive any further forward, the energetic push-back I was feeling would almost be able to physically stop me. I looked out across the sky. There was no rain, but there was some wicked-looking lightning in the clouds ahead. I got another sinking feeling in my gut. I spoke out loud what I was feeling, "We shouldn't be here. We need to turn around and go home."

"What? Why?" Marin asked from the back, Bucky's head laying over her lap.

"I don't know. I'm just getting a feeling that we shouldn't be here, so I am going to listen to my gut." I turned the car around in the middle of the road where we'd stopped and started to head back towards home. Home was fifty-seven minutes away and the camper was three. It made no sense, yet I was not going to ignore this strong, intuitive feeling.

About eight minutes down the road, my phone and Gavin's phone started to go off with the loud alarm of a weather alert. He looked down at his phone in his hand and told me what it said: "Tornado warning. Take cover." *Shit*, I thought, but didn't dare say out loud. The sky was getting darker, and I wondered what to do. I was fighting with myself, *Should I pull over so we can run to a stranger's house for shelter, or should I turn around and head back towards the camper? No*, it felt like *not* to do that, so I just kept driving, saying a prayer under my breath, *God, please protect us and keep us safe.*

We made it to the County Highway 8 stop sign in Turtle Lake a few minutes later. As I sat at the stop sign waiting for the cars on the highway to pass, I thought, *Should I turn left so we can take shelter at the gas station, or do I keep going straight towards home?* I looked at the sky ahead of me and could see some blue peeking through. I looked at the sky behind me; it was a thick gray. I decided to drive towards the blue sky. It felt like if I could see the blue sky and get us closer to it, then we would be safe. So, forward I went, gripping the wheel with tense hands and hoping to God I was making the right moves.

"Mom, are we going to be okay?" Marin asked nervously from the back seat.

"Yes, Marin," I reassured her. "Do you see that blue sky in front of us? That's where we are going, away from the storm. As long as we can see that blue sky, we know we'll be okay." I drove faster now, desperate to leave the gray wall behind and break deeper into the blue sky ahead. We were not five more minutes down the road when the wall cloud overtook us. The blue sky we had been following was blocked from our sight, as if we were suddenly swallowed whole. Heavy wind and torrential rain attacked the soft car top. We were all in full panic mode. I kept driving, not sure if I should pull off the road, not sure if I could keep driving either. The inside of the storm was so black, I could hardly see.

Then, with miraculous timing, we came upon a tiny town with a restaurant gas station. *Hell yes,* I thought to myself as I pulled in. The kids and I, and even Bucky, ran inside to take cover. The power had gone out in the building, but the employees were at the door to let us in, and told us quickly to go in the back storage room where ten other people were already taking shelter. We were shaken and still scared, but feeling a little better in a secure building. We waited out the storm in the dark, my kids huddled close next to me and Bucky in my arms.

After about fifteen minutes, one of the other people was able to get through on his cell phone to his family in Turtle Lake, seven miles away.

"They said a tornado touched down," he reported.

*Oh my gosh.* I immediately thought about how we could have been in the gas station I had decided to pass up. I was so glad that I had chosen to drive farther.

We stayed a bit longer after things had calmed down outside, just to make sure the coast was clear. I called Corey and told him that we had just dodged a tornado, that we were okay, and that we would be heading home. When we did leave, just a few houses down from the restaurant, there were two trees that had been snapped off, twenty feet above the ground. It looked like someone had taken a chainsaw and cut straight through them, but it was the strong winds in the tornado zone that had snapped them clean off. After those trees, I didn't see any more damage. We had made it to the outer edge of the tornado, out of harm's way, and were now driving home safely in disbelief and gratitude.

Later we found out two tornados had actually gone through. One was in Turtle Lake and one further north, near our campground. There ended up being miles and miles of damage: hundreds of trees down, many barns toppled, and roofs pulled off. A couple of campers at our campground had been crushed by falling trees. No one was injured, thank goodness, but the devastation was widespread. I thought then about how it could have been Gavin, Marin, Bucky, and myself alone in the death-tube of a camper, scared shitless in the tornado, and I was so incredibly grateful that that was not what had happened. I was grateful that the still, small voice inside of me and the spiritual help around me had spoken up so that I could hear the warning, make the right turns, and get to where we needed to be to avert danger. Thank God for intuition and for being able to listen to it.

## Intuition's Language

Dodging a tornado is perhaps an extreme example because intuition mostly shows up in commonplace moments. When you tap into intuition, it is your own guiding resource. It is helpful to have the light of inner consciousness to illuminate your way in the world, which can be dim and hard to navigate. There is no capacity that you have, that has been created within you, that was *not* created by God. God is the creator of all. The creation of will, of desire, and of intuition—all of which have the potential to be used purposefully or to be misused. While intuition is a natural, God-given tool, it can most certainly take practice to be able to use it purposefully, and to develop and strengthen it like a God given muscle.

Intuition is the combination of your body and spirit working in unison: its language becomes experienceable as your heart, body, and mind align together in knowing and feeling. You are designed to filter both physical sensations and subtle impressions through intuition in order to *feel* the language of you communicating to you. Intuition as a language is a connector to truth. One intuitive occurrence we previously touched on is when you get goosebumps—they are your spirit-body truth-detector giving you confirmation that something is real or true.

To develop and strengthen your inner guiding light, the practice of experiencing intuition improves your skill in its use. The more you can be aware of how you feel, the more your intuition can be sensed. It can be like changing the dial on the radio—from scrambling static between stations to a channel where you can hear and understand what's being played. Perhaps you might even decide to tune into that station more often, as you enjoy the frequency of picking up on the intricacies of your life.

## Weeding out Falsity to Increase the Light

It is not always easy to decipher what is true intuition and what isn't—just like when talking to others, it is not always easy to discern if they are speaking fact or fiction. Similarly, in your self-connection, the other side of the coin is the inner self-talk that can feed you bite-sized pieces of shit. Yes, there is yet another dualistic and complicated layer to navigate: you have both an inner voice of truth and an inner voice of lies. However, the good thing is that self-awareness not only helps build intuition, but it helps temper dishonest and negative self-talk. Awareness of negative self-talk decreases our succumbing to believing its lies because we start to recognize the narratives for what they are: made-up stories.

Intuition is a frequency of conductive light, and self-talk is a frequency of static interference. Self-intuition lights your way; self-talk can throw shade that leads you off track. But with both being experienced internally and left up to interpretation, neither is a perfectly mapped road. However, in having a closer connection with yourself it can become easier to recognize what is real *vs.* the false reality your inner critic would have you believe. That unhelpful self-talk that beats you up and tears you down, leaving you feeling timid and unmotivated, is a light-stealing illusion that perpetuates disconnection. A helpful practice to counter the convoluted lies of negative self-talk is to be aware when your negative mind is running away with you and to ask yourself, *Am I making this up, or is this real?* The next time you are worrying about something, catch yourself by noticing that you are worrying. Then notice what the story in your mind is saying about your worry. It might look something like this:

*I have not had a call back from the bakery about the price of my son's birthday cake. I bet they have forgotten to make it. I bet the note to call me back to confirm the cost got buried under some papers. I bet they probably just don't care about calling me back. They probably think I am pushy for telling them I needed a call back to confirm the cost. What if they assumed that meant not to make the cake?* Round and round the wheels of the mind go. Until, *Oh, wait. I notice I am really worrying about this. Time for me to examine: am I making this up or is it real? Well, I guess the only thing real is that I did order the cake and asked them to call me back about the price and that was three days ago. I do not know anything else. Instead of spinning myself out through creating worry-stories, I am just going to call them and get to the bottom of things.*

The mind is a great storyteller—sometimes to your own detriment when you weave elaborate stories that are just plain fictitious and sometimes even vicious. It can be very illuminating to shine a light on your mental chatter. With self-awareness, you can explore whether you are creating a story in your mind falsely by taking time to identify the facts. And with self-awareness in intuition, you can also have a conversation and receive helpful insight. To some extent, it is a tandem exploration of probing for falsity and truth.

The dimension of human intelligence that is intuition is important, but when you view intelligence as being only a facet of the mind, then you prevent yourself from being open to integrating the other intelligent faculties intuition involves into your experience. For example, a subtle, intuitive intelligence someone might have is the skill of playing music by ear. They don't need the music written out; they understand sound through other intelligent faculties and can reproduce what they hear with accuracy. This is a kind of subtle, intuitive language.

The dictionary definition of *intuition* defines it as a non-mental intelligence, but fails to explain the source of this intelligence. The source is you, deciphering intelligently through your physical, emotional, and even spiritual awareness, that is integrated with your conscious mental awareness. On Lexico.com, an online dictionary, one definition describes it as, "The ability to understand something immediately, without the need for conscious reasoning." Another definition says, "[Intuition is] a thing that one knows or considers likely from instinctive feeling rather than conscious reasoning." Intuition is not all that hard to understand, but you can't really understand it by thinking about it. You can't really understand it by reading its definition, either: you have to experience it. You have to see and feel it for yourself to understand it. It is the experiencing of it that solidifies it as real and functional.

### Awareness Exercise

Self-intuition is the most accurate mode *vs.* trusting someone else's intuition for yourself. Your intuition actively connects you to yourself and your life so let's get active in practicing it. This exercise is an intuitive tool that you can use when overthinking gets in your way. When you are volleying back and forth between a *do this* or *don't do that* scenario, it can be helpful to take your head out of the game and insert the intelligence of your body. Sometimes it is your feeling sense, grounded in your body, that speaks your truth and gives you a helpful direction. This beginner's exercise will aid you in building multi-faceted, intuitive self-awareness by starting you with being aware of the subtle cues of the body. It is somewhat similar to the previous exercise you did when you said the words *love* and *fear* and felt your inner response.

In this exercise, you are going to make opposing statements on a matter. During saying one of the statements, and in the moment just following it, you will tune in to how it feels when you say it. Then repeat this for the opposite statement. Pay attention to which of the opposing statements makes you feel open and light and which makes you feel closed and heavy. This will lead you to seeing that the answer is in the body. The body's inner wisdom can give you direction through its resistance and its openness. The result indicates that the statement causing you to feel openness is the choice that is most in alignment with you in the moment.

Here is a guide to take you through the first statements. Read through it and then do the exercise:

Statement #1: "I will go to bed tonight at midnight."

Statement #2: "I will go to bed tonight at 10:00 p.m."

○  Keep the first statement in your head, because you will be saying it with your eyes closed in order to closely pay attention to your inner feeling sense.

○  Close your eyes, say #1, and feel your body's response.

○  Now close your eyes, say #2, and feel your body's response.

○  Perhaps do another round of the same statements to tune in again, more deeply. Notice the subtle difference in your body between saying them.

○  Which statement felt less resistant and which felt more open in your body?

Here is another set of statements to say and tune in with:

Statement #1: "I will spend $50 on groceries."

Statement #2: "I will spend $50 on bubble gum."

And another:

Statement #1: "I will walk up the stairs blind-folded, with my hands tied behind my back."

Statement #2: "I will walk up the stairs with my eyes open and my hands free."

Now feel free to make up your own statements and give it a go. Write them down so both statements are in an affirmative sentence. You are not asking yes or no questions, but stating a definite and picking up on the subtle cues that follow. Maybe pick something you need to decide. It can be something big or something little like, *I will eat spaghetti for dinner vs. I will eat soup for dinner.* Play with it and notice what you feel.

The differences in how your body responds to the opposing statements can be subtle, but they are present. It's all about learning to sense tiny cues of inner knowingness. The ability to read yourself is a skill, a tool, and a gift. Like a funnel, it takes all of the information being received and siphons it down to a clearer stream of consciousness. Think of a speaker reading their audience and gauging in the moment whether to lengthen or shorten their speech, *Yup, this feels right for this situation,* or, *Nope, that doesn't feel right here.* We can function on the fly because our intuitive ability gives us the capacity to do so, to discern subtle cues, and to make fitting decisions.

## Listening to the Heart

From the moment I got the call that my husband was in cardiac arrest, my own heart seized up. I could feel it immediately tighten inside my chest, and it didn't let go. In the days that followed his dying, it was still tight like a vice. In moments where I held my hand against my heart to soothe it, I could not believe how much physical pain there was. It felt like there really might be a wound slashed deep across my heart. I now know that having a broken heart is a real thing. But this was not *just* physical pain, it was an echo through my body of the emotional pain and the pain of separation from my heart's great love. My heart kept beating, but it was compromised in bracing against feeling this deep heartache. As the months stretched on, I continued to have this physical heartache. I frequently had tightness and pain in the center of my chest, at my energetic heart center, and also in my heart organ to the left. It was no condition a doctor would diagnose, yet I knew that because my body and emotions are undividable, it was no less of a real ailment.

My knowledge in the interconnectedness of disease across body, emotion, mind, and spirit comes from my background as a trained energy therapist since 2009. I have witnessed in myself and in others, how energy therapy is able to reach non-physical places of holding that would otherwise not be reachable. So, I sought treatment for my heartache, afraid that if I let it go on, it could lead to other problems like anxiety, panic attacks, arrhythmia, or heart disease later in life.

In one energy therapy session, I was guided to focus on exploring this heart pain in the wake of processing my grief. Naomi, who is an occupational therapist but is also trained in AcuEnergetics®, Craniosacral therapy, and Shamanism, had her healing hands placed over my heart and instructed me to go into where I was feeling the pain. "Ask the pain how can it be helped," she suggested. She too knows that the body has its own intelligence and its own language that we can hear with internal listening.

When I asked my body the question by repeating it in my mind, the answer that came was: *movement.* And then I got a mental image: me standing with weights in my hands and my arms pumping up and down. I could hear the words in my head and feel my body respond to what it was telling me: *I need to step it up.* I needed to get my blood pumping, to give my heart some good energy-flowing cardio by stepping up my physical activity, which then would support movement of my emotional energy in the heart, too. It makes sense, right? Exercising any muscle loosens it up, expels pent-up energy, and strengthens it. Getting in some cardio, getting my blood and heart pumping in healthy circulation, would create energetic flow for the physical *and* emotional stagnation of my heart to move. Prior to this, I had never thought about getting my heart pumping to help move my grief. It was a new and solid direction for me in my heart's healing journey. And it came from simply talking to, and listening directly to, my heart.

It is possible for you to also receive answers like this by engaging in an open dialogue of asking questions of yourself. And how will you hear the reply? Again, through self-awareness and openness.

## Awareness Exercise

You have already learned one way of using intuition for what feels right or best in the opposing statements exercise. Another way of being tapped in is when information just pops into your awareness. This can happen randomly because if you are dialed into the station, well, you are dialed into the station. It can also happen on-demand by connecting through a verbal conversation with your inner knowingness in which you listen for a reply.

There are four ways that subtle language comes through into intuitive communication. They are: visually seeing in your mind's eye, hearing in your mind's ear, feeling in your multisensory body, and cognizant knowing. These cover the dimensions of what are called the four *clairs*. *Claircognizance* is mental, *clairsentience* is physical and or emotional feeling, *clairvoyance* is seeing, and *clairaudience* is hearing. Interestingly, the word *clair* means "clear"—it's like getting rid of the static in order to decipher clearly your multi-input. You can use these four ways of tuning in to self-dialogue for your benefit; noticing how your inner compass is guiding you in goodness.

For this exercise, you will start with quieting down by closing your eyes and feeling your breath. Then you will ask a question and listen for a reply. It is important to learn how to tune in to your internal self *vs.* being distracted by the ever-present outside world. Feeling the breath is a natural way to tune in; as you feel your breath, you naturally attune to feeling yourself. In doing so, you can amplify awareness of those varying ways in which the channels of intuition speak from within you—paying attention to visuals, feelings, or thoughts. Just being open creates the potential for the connection to be made and communication to be received. There is no need to try too hard or second-guess yourself; just take what comes in with playful curiosity.

Now for the exercise:

○ Quiet yourself by closing your eyes and feeling your breath for a minute or so.

○ Next, keeping eyes closed, direct your attention to go to your heart, asking it simply, *Heart, what is it you want me to know?* Notice what comes in reply.

○ Record your experience in your journal.

○ Plan to come back another day and do this exercise again and also record it then.

Let's also take it a step further in connecting this exercise to a person in your life.

○ Again, close your eyes and feel your breath. Center and tune in.

○ Now, put your attention in your heart and ask, *Heart, what is it you want me to know about my relationship with ____?* And notice what comes to you in reply.

○ Record any impressions in your journal.

Please remember this is practice not perfection. As a beginner, it can take time to hear the subtle language. Sometimes, it can be hard to decipher the information. Is it true intuition or just self-talk? It is not a perfect science but an exploratory art of inner knowingness. A connection to your inner wisdom. Feel free to create your own practice and see how the connection and communication can develop.

## Time for Insight

To end this chapter, it would be helpful to gather some insight based on how you feel about yourself at this time. From a generalized perspective rate on a scale of 0 to 10 whether you feel that you are overall a hindrance to yourself or a help. The 0 being extreme hindrance and 10 being an extreme help. As you think about this, trust whatever number pops into your mind as a gut instinct response. This broad encompassing rating gives you a sense of the current quality of connection in your self-relationship.

Additional self-probing questions:

o   *What am I struggling with about myself?*

o   *What am I strong in?*

o   *What do I spend more time in connection with, my strength or my struggle?*

o   *Am I more connected to the part of me that feels strong or the part that feels weak?*

o   *How do my answers relate to the rating in Chapter 1 of how connected I feel to myself and my view now of if I am a help or a hinder?*

Being with yourself all the time does not mean you are in alignment with yourself. Your answers are reflective of where you are or are not in alignment with where you want to be. Nobody really wants to hinder themselves. Everyone has an inner desire to be their best self because, really, who wants to be a shitty version of themselves? I'm guessing this motivation is what inspired you to pick up this book. So, while these questions may be difficult to answer, answering them is pivotal to learn more about yourself so that you can feel more connected to who you are and where you are going. So, thank yourself now for your self-honesty and for your bravery.

## Connection Practices

Full disclosure to yourself starts with knowing you don't have to know everything, do everything, or be everything. You are only fully able to be exactly where you are right now and that is enough. In fact, it is perfect. In the openness of your heart to be where you are right now and *feel* into where you are, you have opened the potential for using your own actions to *shift up and out* of any stuck patterning that keeps repeating like a worn-out broken record. You have begun breathing new life into a healthy and supportive self-relationship. And good news for you: your inner light was never turned off. In any darkness you may have experienced or be experiencing, your light was there. It is there for you now. You are your own light, and you are fully able to turn that glow up and light up your life with it. The following are two practices that will aid turning your light up through illuminating healthy connection with yourself.

1.   Self-care is a healthy *must* because it is healthy across all dimensions of your being mind, body, emotion, and spirit. It is a sort of dusting off and amplifying of your light. A force that aids in flipping the coin of duality from a life that wears and tears you down to a life that refreshes you and builds you up. Feel good stuff to do just that, make you feel good and make you feel good about yourself.

2.   The practice of stillness is also helpful in connecting with yourself by lighting up your awareness. You can't be aware of how you are if you never give yourself a chance to intimately and quietly *be* with yourself, just like you can't hear what is being said if you're talking all the time. You must be both the active, yang sender and passive, yin receiver in your relationship with yourself. Stillness gives you this space. A fabulous practice in stillness is the meditation of feeling the breath. This was touched on earlier—sitting quietly and feeling the breath. Start by doing it for fifteen minutes a day for two weeks and see what goodness starts to show up for you in settling in to this practice. Then you can take it even further and do it for life.

Do not underestimate yourself. You have the capacity to be both a beautiful catalyst and a crushing destroyer in your life. Self-awareness is your best friend, and honesty is its glowing counterpart. If you can see your dark corners and shaded areas, that is a *good* thing. The more aware you are, the less unconsciously you are living your life. We must each have the courage to look at ourselves unfiltered, to admit our flaws and our strengths. Because the honest truth is if you are living and breathing, you have both. Perfectly imperfect, as they say; another yin-and-yang thing. Nobody is spared from errors and mistakes. No one is spared from pain and challenge. Luckily, at the exact same time, we all are endowed with the gift of growth, the gift of triumph, the gift of overcoming as best as we can. And we are all afforded the opportunity to love, to forgive, and to have compassion. Those are God-given gifts of the heart that you are *not* supposed to hold back from gifting to yourself. So, look to the light and shine on, you bright beauty.

"Look up child,

Look up."

–Lauren Daigle, "Look Up Child"

# 4

# FROM INNER TO OUTER

## *Your Relationship with Others*

If a raindrop that falls into the ocean viewed itself as man views himself,

the raindrop would then be a drop of water trapped in an ocean;

when in reality, the raindrop is the ocean.

—Craig Smedley

Imagine your day starts with your alarm ringing. You reach to turn it off and awaken to your day. The first person you see is someone who lives with you. As you see them, you have a question pop up to ask them. They do not respond well. Words, looks, and energy are exchanged but the day is moving forward, so you need to get going. You have lingering thoughts running through your head as you leave and they are not nearly as sweet as the latte will be that you are heading to get.

When you get to the coffee shop, there is a line. You are due at work in fifteen minutes and are instantly irritated as you hear the woman three people in front of you, with two kids, telling them to, "Make up your mind."

You feel a little heat rush to your face in anger now and think, *Lady, why'd you even get in line if you weren't ready to order?* As you sigh impatiently, the man in front of you turns around and gives you a look like, *What's her problem?* You're a little embarrassed. Finally, the line moves and you are up to order, "Two caramel lattes please."

Coffees in hand, you rush out of the shop and bump into your favorite coworker. "Good morning," she says with a welcoming smile.

"Here, I got you a coffee," you say as the two of you enter the building together.

"Thank you so much, you are so sweet," she says with appreciation. "Ready for today's meeting?"

Your stomach sinks with fear as you know the meeting is going to be about restructuring the company. You have been worrying for days that your position is being eliminated. "As ready as I'll ever be," you quip.

You have a few minutes before the meeting starts, so you quickly check your phone. You read a text from your neighbor and friend who says she has decided to sell her house and move. *Where is this coming from?* You think in confusion. You feel instantly sad and disappointed.

Finally, the meeting starts. Your boss speaks the words you have been dreading, "Your position is being eliminated." Your heart jumps up into your throat and you feel like you could vomit. A short pause and he continues: "That is why I have decided to promote you to an executive role." You instantly tear up in surprise and joy. What a day. And it's only 8:10 a.m.

While this isn't really *your* life, this is life—with other people in it. It can be smooth sailing one moment and a bumpy rollercoaster another. Life is colorful because it is colored by the people in it—with their personalities, moods, and quirks. Their many colors shade our many emotions, as well; sometimes they darken us a hue, and sometimes they brighten us.

## Interconnection: Same Fabric, Different Designs

People are *a part of* your experience of life, they are not separate from it. You are a part of the experience other people have of life, too. The interactions you have with people shape your experience of living. You make an impression upon them, either consciously or unconsciously, and they on you. Have you ever had to deal with a rude person, an inconsiderate driver, or maybe been seated near a stranger's screaming child? Have you ever carried that experience forward with you, soured and tense? You are not so separate from the interactions you field on a daily basis.

If life is an ocean, we each are a molecule of water within it. All people are linked in relationship in this way. However, we live in individual bodies, with individual eyes viewing through the perspective that we are separate from each other. The human experience is both being part of the whole *and* an individual, at the same time. Like an endless tapestry that goes out in all directions, you have your own shape and color as an individual thread, but you are woven into the same fabric that all others are also woven into. Relationship is a good illustrator of this interconnection because it takes two people together to make it, and together, the two blend into one relationship. You are not *in* a relationship; you *are* the relationship. It's a fully integrated experience of internal to external. However, where you focus can impact the amount of connectedness and the quality of the connection, too. In fact, how you are with others externally reflects back to you how you are within yourself. It ends up that your interactions make up a real part of your baseline of openness or closedness in life.

> If we have no peace, it is because we have
>
> forgotten that we belong to each other.
>
> −Mother Teresa

## The Single Side of Experience

We have "forgotten that we belong to each other" because of our single-sided view. Generally speaking, *you* are the focal point of all of your interactions. You absorb the impression of how each interaction plays out and then all you can do to navigate it is to act from within yourself. You cannot control the other person. Manipulation is a sign of being out of control *vs.* being in control, so that doesn't count either.

Sometimes a positive or a negative interaction sticks with you for quite a while and colors your day, creating a domino effect for how the rest of the day will fall. And that is because there is an energy exchanged in your interactions. Even though you *have* a single view you *are* an energy sponge, and the problem with your sponginess, soaking in others' energy and leaching out your own, is that you are never in a clear playing field. Your self-conduct is very related to not only your character and qualities but those of the people you interact with. Negative influences can come at you in the form of eye daggers, disappointing or hurtful words, or overly opinionated sharing to name a few. And these things impacting you can sometimes *catch you* and run away with you instead of you catching them by being aware of how they are coloring your view of the day.

Sometimes in having a single-sided view you can be too self focused; sometimes the problem is that you are not self-focused enough. But I hope that you can realize that you need both: to be self-focused *and* focused on others. And you need others to do the same: to focus on themselves while being attentive to you. There is a balance; each way of being balances the other from being extreme. Being self-focused does not necessarily mean a person is selfish. And being absorbed in others does not necessarily benefit you or them. It is best to let an awareness of both yourself and others be a part of your single-sided view because the two awarenesses together feed into the one thing shared between you: the quality of your relationship. The inner and outer awareness combine and equate to the relationship's level of meaningful impact.

## The Danger of Aloneness

A wedge that has been driven into my conscious experiencing of late is the striking difference between the others in my life and me. I look around at all of my close friends, all of mine and Corey's extended friendships, at the parents of our children's friends, at my family, and I am the only one who is alone. I am the only single parent in the mix of people who have been in our lives since the days when we were still an *us*. It's just the way it is. I can be thankful I am surrounded by good people in strong relationships and, at the same time, it hurts. I want that to still be *us*. In weaker and harsher moments,

I allow it to be a dimension of my pain. It is something outside of myself that pours salt on the wound within me. That is just where I am in the now.

Salt, however, has healing properties. It cleanses and supports healing. So, I take the pain in the stark difference that I feel, and I look to building new relationships outside of what is. I have recognized my need to have people in my life that I can relate to. I need to build relationship with those who are grieving, who are single, who are widows, who are solo-parenting. And, I have been able to connect with such people in both the face-to-face and the virtual world. I have become a part of a local Widowed And Young (WAY) group that meets a handful of times a year for dinner where we share life experience and support in our various stages of widowhood. I am a part of a Facebook group for young widows that is an open forum to hear others and to be heard, with helpful feedback and understanding both given and received. I am connecting with others similar to me during this stage of rebuilding what my life *will be* from where my life *has been*. In my self-focus of being aware of my needs, I have made room for new people. Finding it supportive to honor where I am by allowing meaningful connection to expand.

This need to assess what your needs are and grow in your relationships can come about from varying life circumstances. Like a change in the location of where you live, where you work, or where you attend school. Or it might stem from life changes like exploring faith, or bettering yourself in wellness interests, or even in recovery of some sort, perhaps from addiction or illness. In all of these examples, you can benefit hugely by surrounding yourself with people in similar walks of life as you. Are you taking on a new project, maybe home renovation, or are you starting down the entrepreneurial path? All of the above are opportune times to expand and seek relationships that complement your unique needs surfacing in a unique time. It is possible to find your self-focused needs fulfilled in external relationship.

The other end of the self-focus viewpoint spectrum is when you get stuck in the feeling of being separate from everybody else and thus see yourself as alone. Feeling alone can be debilitating and dangerous for your well-being. Feeling alone is one of the most crippling emotions for human beings because it goes against the very grain of what you were designed for: being in relationship. In aloneness, there is often hopelessness and desperation—this is why *feeling* alone is different than *being* alone. Every person needs doses of being alone to connect with himself or herself. In being alone in this way, there is contentment: it is a healthy space to be in. But *feeling* alone is a signal that there is a lack of connection in relationship. That your current state of relationship is not meeting your need and is not emotionally sustaining you. That is unhealthy because your need for connection is not being fulfilled, and that creates a hole in being able to feel your own wholeness.

The inner self-focus can take over and make it hard to hear beyond the thoughts of aloneness in your mind. It can stunt you from reaching out, from being there for others, and even from letting others be there for you. But those perpetuating thoughts are doing something else, too. They are giving you an indicator that you need to seek connection. You are not really alone. Or at least, you don't have to be. Whether you feel connected to others or not, there are people around you. Whether or not you are currently connected to others who have similar views or experiences to you, there are others somewhere out there like you. The only counterbalance to loneliness is other people.

One of the greatest catalysts to self-growth is also other people. Through good or bad, others inspire our growth. Positive interactions nourish us, while negative ones break us down. But even in destruction, growth still shows up in that it can make us stronger. Sometimes, with that strength gained, we are then able to be the catalyst to help build that relationship to be stronger, too. Sometimes a relationship doesn't need to be tossed aside—it needs to be dug into and cultivated to grow. This is because growth is made possible not only through positive interactions but also in getting through negative ones.

When muscle is built, the very fibers that hold it together get shredded apart. But then a miracle happens, and there is an innate capacity to repair in the face of destruction. The result is a bigger, stronger muscle. And you, like a muscle, have an innate capacity to repair and grow stronger. Furthermore, negative relationship experiences can also make you more sympathetic and compassionate. In having your negative experiences, you have shared in the human experience. You can relate to others through your joys, yes, but also through your pains.

People need each other—and not just because we were created in the duality of symbiotic relationships, in which each relationship is defined by the difference marked by *otherness*. For example, you *vs.* me, us *vs.* them, or the individual *vs.* the collective. You also need others because you are multidimensional. Others help fulfill your needs on all levels: physically, emotionally, mentally, and spiritually. We need others outside of us to communicate to us: I see you. I hear you. I feel you. I know you. I love you. Because there is an innate need fulfilled in simply being witnessed and acknowledged.

## The Human Need for Attention

We exist in an ocean of people and just as the ocean needs every drop of water to make up its wholeness, we are each a small part of the larger whole. Paradoxically, our individual wholeness too, is made by being a part of that something bigger, together. Having a true sense of this oneness might transcend our immediate awareness but it is none-the-less woven into our spirit in the way in which people *need* other people to solidify feeling whole. Who are you if you are not somebody to someone? You are nobody, and that does not feel whole—but empty. We feel connected to wholeness when we are witnessed for being the individual that we are amongst the sea of people we are floating in. This is why we seek attention in our relationships with others. Attention is the food of our relational multidimensionality. You are fed by spiritual, emotional, physical, and mental attention. You have an appetite for it, you crave it, and it nourishes you. Through attention, you are encouraged by an outer presence pressing up against you so that you can both *know* you are alive and *feel* alive. Without others, part of who you are meant to be is dimmed.

Standing in the driveway on a warm and sunny day in May, I can hear four tires whizzing around on the blacktop of our driveway.

"Mom, watch this," Gavin says, as he tries to pop a wheelie on his blue mountain bike. He tries to keep it up on one wheel as he rides over the seam lines in the cement. He has mastered staying up long enough to pass over two lines and has had some success with making three, and now he wants to show me what he is trying for. I watch as his front wheel pops up and his legs keep pedaling, moving him forward over one… two… and the front wheel comes down just before the third line.

He whips his bike around to go back to his starting point, calling, "Watch me again."

While keeping my eyes on him, I hear the two other wheels coming up behind me from the front sidewalk. Marin is rolling in on her scooter. "Mom, watch me do a trick."

"Hang-on." I tell her, "I am watching your brother."

Gavin tries again and is just short. "One more time, Mom."

I call to him, "Hang on. Marin wants me to watch her for a minute too."

With eyes now on Marin, she begins her scooter routine. Her left foot touches down upon the pavement and pushes off. As she gains speed and rolls away, she moves in a figure-eight pattern in the driveway. She stretches her left leg up and out to the side and glides forward on her scooter as she arches her back and tilts her chin up to the sky.

"Nice." I say, acknowledging her and then turning back to Gavin.

"Are you watching?" he asks.

"Yes." I say, eyes on him. He builds up speed then leans back, popping his tire up and rolling over one… two… three lines. His front wheel comes down and he instantly looks at me with a huge grin.

"Did you see that, Mom?"

At the same time, Marin asks, "Mom, can you watch me again?" My attention continues to ping back and forth between my children as I watch their trials and successes.

Their need for me to witness and acknowledge what they are doing is not limited to the driveway alone but spreads across every single day. One could liken attention to being another energetic currency that gets exchanged, like language. Language is a basic human tool, but attention is a basic human need that we naturally seek to be fulfilled. I recognize this innate need through my children. It is a simple yet constant need. Ever since they were little, they sought for my attention. Thousands and thousands of times, I've heard them call out, "Mom, Mom, look at me. Watch me." They are hungry for me to look up from my task and be present with them. To see them and acknowledge them in what they are doing.

The desire to be seen and acknowledged stands out from my own childhood, too. Nearly, every day of the summer, my mom would take my brother, Ryan, and me to my Grandma Slanker's house. While they were busy in the garden or kitchen, we would get to swim in my grandparents' in-ground pool. Occasionally, Mom and Grandma would come out with a glass of iced tea and sit by the pool. This always resulted in Ryan and I doing tricks to show off, calling to her, "Hey Mom, watch me. Look at me. See what I can do." The apple does not fall far from the tree. We all need attention.

## Time for Insight

Can you think of a time in your life when you yearned for someone to see you? Were you seen by that other person in that instance?

If you answered *yes*, write down what happened when you were seen. How did it make you feel?

If you answered *no*, write down what happened when you weren't seen? How did it make you feel?

Now think of another time that fits the opposite outcome that you just recalled and reflect on what happened then—after the *yes* or the *no*, how did you feel?

## The Energy of Attention

Attention is a currency exchanged that has value because it makes you feel that you have value. It has a certain quality that is palpable and fulfilling. If you think about it, this human need for connection and attention is actually what has fueled the massive growth of social media. When others witness you, it feels good and is validating. Who doesn't feel good when given a genuine compliment or acknowledgment of a job well done? (If compliments don't make you feel good about yourself, take note of that. There is a disconnect somewhere to weed out.) Having openness in connection allows you to both give and receive attention and fosters a sense of belonging.

People seek attention consciously and unconsciously, in positive and negative ways. Even though attention is a basic need, it is still dynamic and dualistic. Not all attention is good attention. Sometimes people give attention with ill-intentions, such as manipulation and sabotage, and sometimes with good intentions, such as care and kindness. Some people exude negative energy in order to attract attention. Some exude positive energy for the same reason. It is complicated. When attention is rooted in light it can open you up; yet attention shrouded in darkness diminishes your openness. Because of the complexity of seeking and getting attention, having this need met can sometimes be a slippery slope.

You learn things about yourself in your relationships by how others interact with you: when attention is given for the right reasons, it fosters connection with that person but also helps you to see yourself. For example, if you take the time to help an elder with lawn care and they send you a touching thank you card, this reinforces that you are helpful and considerate. When attention is based off of falsity, highlighting something you are not, then it can have a disconnecting effect. An example of this is verbal abuse where someone may be saying awful things about you, to you. Sometimes you can be tricked into thinking the hurtful statements may be true. However, the real truth is that when a jerk acts like a jerk, it says *more* about them than about you. In situations like this the one thing that it should really be teaching you about yourself is that you don't deserve to be treated like that.

For your whole life, you will be both a student and a teacher simultaneously. This is because connection is the conduit between your inner experience of self and the outer world of others. Think of a time that you too may have been treated poorly by someone. Unknowingly, the poorly acting person is the teacher for you, but they too have the potential to learn from the situation—to be the student. Perhaps they come back to it in their own mind later and realize that they could have handled it differently—now they are the student and you the teacher.

Teachable moments can take time to mature and blossom. Sometimes you might not understand or see them right away. But eventually, if you are open to seeing the silver lining, you will. And eventually, if someone else is meant to receive your casting light, they will. You can only plant the seeds. You can't force the teachings to grow. Yielding a fruitful lesson-learned takes time. Others can inspire this inner gestation and you can inspire it in others. No matter the time it takes, keep planting your seeds of goodness, light, and connection.

## We Need Support from Others

My mom first got cancer when I was fifteen and she was forty-six. It was breast cancer, which showed up as abnormal tissue in her left breast. Hearing the c-word for the first time in relation to my dear mother, I couldn't help but question, *Is she going to die?* Life-and-death fear comes in quickly when the possibility of death shows up. During her treatment, she was so stoic in facing her cancer battle and stayed her sweet self. I remember her being the same cute Mom, tapping her toes and singing a song as she stood in the kitchen, working over dishes or food. Life was strong in her, which afforded me the luxury of believing she was going to be okay.

The second time my mom's cancer showed up in her body, I was about seventeen years old. I completely closed down. This time, it was more dire because it was the *second* time. That meant her first treatment was not successful enough to keep her in remission for the rest of her life. Fears returned and emotionally I froze. I didn't tell anyone. I didn't talk about it to my friends. I didn't let anyone in to bear witness to what my family and I were going through. I think it was too real and scary to face, so I ignored it. I went to school quiet and cold. I locked it all up inside. I stuffed it down and covered it over with sadness and withdrawal. But in trying to ignore it, it crushed me anyway.

One day, sitting underneath the white pines that lined my friend Connor's backyard, I broke down. "My mom has to shave her head again," I said. "And the chemo is upsetting her stomach. I am so scared to think about what if, this time, she can't fight it."

Big tears fell, and I covered up my face with my hands, embarrassed to let him see me cry so hard. Then big, warm arms wrapped around me and pulled me in close. "I am so sorry," he said. And he just let me cry, as long and as hard as I needed to. He let me let it out. Eventually things came to light, and the news spread to all my friends. That's one of the best things about friends: they show up when you need them. In letting myself be vulnerable about how I was feeling inside, I was able to learn that I needed their support. Also, allowing myself to be open with them translated into more openness with myself—an openness of accepting and living the reality of mom's cancer and her treatment. This was a healthier way to be processing and navigating what I couldn't change but desperately wished I could.

Having connections with good people can't entirely save you from yourself, though. They can keep shining their sunshine of encouragement on you, but only *you* can allow yourself to open to the light in seeing a brighter way. If you are dealing with something too heavy that you think you can't share about, don't trust that lie in your head. *You need to share about it with someone.* In doing so, you can lift a ton of bricks off of your shoulders by simply opening your mouth. You will feel better after letting off some of the load on a trusted person. Who knows what other help they might lend you aside from their caring listening ear.

You cannot operate in a vacuum. Who you are in yourself and through yourself is intricately braided into your relationships with others. Sometimes your role in your own relationships can be like a toxic anchor, sinking you further and further down, and sometimes you can be the tugboat that pulls yourself happily along. From your tugboat, you can see you are surrounded by people to grab hold of the ropes and help you move forward, if you let them. How you are in your relationships often is directional to where you are going within them.

## Inner Openness in You Promotes Outer Openness in Others

Another few years had passed when I got the crushing news again. I was home for Christmas break from college in Eau Claire. I had moved out there only four months before, transferring college from Michigan to Wisconsin to be closer to Corey to see if what we had been feeling for each other over the last two years was real. As I sat in the family room of the home I had grown up in, Grandpa Joe stopped by from next door for a visit. He sat in a chair at the dining room table with my dad and hung his head low. Usually, Grandpa Joe's visits involved cussing about politics and banging his fist on the table, so I instantly noticed the lack of his normally loud and boisterous demeanor. My mom sat in her rocking chair on the edge of the family room near the dining room and did not get up.

"That cancer, once it gets you, it's hard to get away from," he said. As I continued to listen to his talk with my dad, my heart broke. It was in that indirect conversation that I learned my sweet, strong mom's cancer was back and had spread to her bone and brain.

As soon as Grandpa Joe left, I got up from the couch, went to the rocking chair, and sat on Mom's lap, like a frightened little girl. I hadn't done that since I was six years old. I cried and nestled my face against her shoulder as she put her arms around me and said, "That is not how I wanted you to find out."

My mom had, I thought, just fought through another round of cancer treatment successfully earlier that fall. I had believed she was in remission again for the third time. What I didn't know was that the improvements she had made were not complete. The doctor needed to give her body a break from the chemo so the plan had been to get through the holidays and then reassess in January to see what the situation was. So, just before I was to leave to head back to college, Mom and Dad had had that devastating meeting and found out that they needed to let the rest of the family know that there was still some cancer left in her body.

My loving and supportive parents did not want me to forgo schooling; and so, at the end of Christmas break, I headed back to Eau Claire. Mom chose to fight the cancer again and began treatment. I had both hope and fear surrounding the unknown of what she was really facing. By the middle of February, though, what I had been fearing became the reality: her cancer was terminal. The closeness of death was unknown.

My parents shared over the phone, "It could be a year."

"The tumor has shrunk some with treatment," Mom said trying to reassure me. It was my mom's nature to want to protect me from the pain. She also did not want to disrupt my life, so she insisted that I continue with school and not come home. Despite the normalcy she was trying to hold steady for me, I still felt the situation was very real. I had no choice but to honestly and sadly accept what my mom and our whole family was facing. I could hear over the phone that her voice was changing, but I couldn't see the change taking place in her body as the cancer was slowly taking her down.

Then one day, while I was sitting in my dorm room, two of my best girlfriends from high school, Fran and Maxine, called me. I had established greater openness and honesty with them over the years, so they knew that they could be open and honest with me. While we were talking on the three-way call they said, "We think you'd better come home."

Nobody else had told me that. My mom would have never asked me to leave school. But that's exactly what I needed to do: get home to my dying mom. In doing so, I was gifted to be with her and care for her through the last month of her life. She died on April 14th, Good Friday, 2001. I was twenty-one years old and motherless.

There are some things in life that can be really hard to talk about. But when you speak with openness, you invite openness back to you. That can be all that is needed to make the uncomfortable comfortable and bring the relationship to the next level of dependability. In having healthy and honest connections, you create relationships that have your best interest in mind. Sometimes it is the others in your life that can see for you when you can't see for yourself. And sometimes you do need to take their advice.

## Shared Experience is a Source of Connection

Make new friends, but keep the old.

Those are silver, these are gold.

–Joseph Parry

It can be great to make new friends. Interacting with people through shared interest activities opens this possibility. Being in the same place with the same people repeatedly is a great space to create new friendships. Examples of places to make new friends could be at a gym or at yoga, meditation, or exercise classes. Attending sporting events, concerts, musical jam sessions, or joining a theater. Signing up to be in a bowling, golf, or card league. Finding a crafting or quilting circle. Being a member of a volunteer group. Traveling or camping in new places, surrounded by new people—the possibilities are endless. Shared experience can cater to your personal interests or curiosities while fostering connection and growth.

The reason that shared experience fosters connection is that humans are empathic beings. People feel what others feel along with them. For example, if you are a Green Bay Packers fan and you are in a room with other passionate Packers fans watching the game, you are feeling that vibe. Sharing the experience *and* the feeling makes it easier to connect to them, even if you don't know them, because you are sharing in the same experience on the outside and the inside. It's a powerful, innate mechanism that illustrates how the energy of emotion is transferred from person to person. Not only are you a witness, but you feel what you are a witness to. You, as that drop of water in the ocean, feel the same rippling vibration as others. This connectivity is what makes you get teary when you see someone else cry. This connectivity is what gives you goosebumps when you hear a touching song. This connectivity is what gives you the inner ambition to reach out and offer help to someone in need. It is a beautiful mechanism. You *feel* them. You feel *for* them, *inside of you.*

## Connection to Others Moves Your Growth Forward

Soon after the birth of our son, my husband and I began living in our new house, in our new neighborhood. I connected with a couple of other new moms from the neighborhood, Elise and Irene, and we started building a friendship. The original commonality that brought us together was motherhood. But the thing that solidified our closeness was intuition and connection with spirit. It was something I am not sure if any of us saw coming but was most certainly divinely orchestrated. The timing of these opportunities was meeting me in a place in my life where I was entering the next level of my personal development and ongoing maturation. I was solid in where my life was with my husband and as a family unit. God knew I was now ready to add in some self-growth and begin laying another foundation of support that I would need to draw from in the years to come. He moved the right people into my life in a way I could never have dreamt up myself.

Together, Elise, Irene, and I began going to the weekly intuition classes I spoke of earlier. In these classes, I started to develop an understanding of intuition and energy that would be foundational for the life God was taking me towards. My circle of friends grew bigger as we got to know the other regulars, too. Together, we learned how to listen to and trust that still, small voice. We learned how to hear and see and feel with the subtle senses of our body's intuition. We learned about crystals, chakras, and hands-on healing and practiced on each other. We learned about the spirit world, how it overlaid our own physical world, and that the two worlds were really one. We learned how to connect with, speak to, and hear God, the angels, and lost loved ones. It was a time of transformational growth and life-changing friendships. I felt I was growing more into myself, a self I had never known before. I was encouraged to blossom by the collective light created through being a part of such an incredible group of women.

Having others in your life not only gives you space for connection, it gives you opportunity. Through connections you are given the opportunity to have new experiences, learn new things, and show up in ways that were not previously available to you. You never know how the dots are going to connect when it comes to the changing roles of the people in your life. So never be afraid to let old relationships shift; in the change of scenery, there is a fresh space for something new to arrive, perhaps divinely orchestrated. The people in your life might be bringing you opportunities that you cannot move forward on your path without.

## Variety in Relationships

We all have relationships that are good and inspire goodness in us. And sometimes there are relationships that are bad and inspire the opposite. Then there are the in-between ones that are neither good nor bad and the ones that are a mix of both good and bad. In the different blends of relationship we must have a space within us that is okay with not being everyone's cup of tea. Sometimes the chemistry just does not mix well.

Just because you are not for everyone and everyone is not for you, does not mean that *you* are not good or that *they* are not good. Remember the two sayings: *opposites attract* and *birds of a feather flock together.* Well, even though they are opposite statements, both are true. The negative of these statements also hold up as true: *sometimes opposites don't mix well* and *sometimes people who are too similar don't mix well.* However, when you encounter differences in relationship, be aware that comparison can lead you to get stuck in closed-mindedness. Instead, acceptance is the way to an illuminated heart. And I don't mean acceptance as in taking what is someone else's and making it your own. I mean, taking what is someone else's and letting it be theirs. You know, accepting them. When you say to someone, *I can respect that for you even if I don't accept it for myself* there is fluidity and flexibility to move through differing opinions without giving them too much weight to sink you.

When you compare, you are putting yourself at odds and into a state of duality. When you accept, you are bigger than duality—you are in the flow of connection because you are in acceptance with yourself and others. There is no need to compare. Comparing is only signaling that you feel lack within yourself. Variety and uniqueness are God-given gifts. Even when you do not have the eyes to see the unique beauty of another, your task then is to be mature and respectful.

It is a simple belief...

We are all of one human life.

We must live in harmony with each other.

—Old Hopi proverb

## Time for Insight

In relationships with others, just as in relationship with yourself, you can be a helper or a hinderer, a toxin or a medicine. But remember with human complexity, it is never only one way. Even within the same relationship, you can be both a toxin and a medicine, at different times. This is the back-and-forth expansion and contraction of being wholly human, flawed for glory. How you are towards others is reflective of how you are inside. You can use this relational information to uncover and work through pain so that you can be gentler on the outside because you became gentler on the inside.

Take some time to look at your relationships with others and gauge how you are doing in them.

- *How do I feel about myself in relation to others right now?*
- *Do I feel built up or torn down in my relationships?*

    o   *Are these feelings coming from an inner source, like my mind, or are they from an outer source, like someone else's behavior?*

Now write down a list of a few relationships that can be toxic for you. Then ask yourself:

    o   *How am I toxic in these relationships?*

    o   *What might taking accountability for my toxic behavior look like? And how might that be helpful?*

    o   *How do I deal with hurt?*

    o   *Does this promote connection or disconnection?*

Now make a list of relationships that can be medicine. Then ask yourself:

    o   *How am I medicine in them?*

    o   *What does my medicinal behavior offer to the other person? How might this also be benefiting me?*

The information that you mine from digging deep into yourself is valuable. You are pulling things into your awareness. The medicines are the jewels that emerge already sparkly and shining. The hindrances are the jewels that don't yet look like jewels because they need to be chipped away at and polished to reveal the inner beauty that you have yet to discover in them. When jewels form in the earth, it takes time for crystallization to happen before they grow into a precious gem. This process is not unlike your own, with many different colors and compositions of relationship that are in varying places of their development. It takes time for a true gem to form. So be patient and gentle with yourself. Shine in the areas where you already shine like a medicine. Take note of where you are a hindrance and work in those areas too, learning as you go. All will be alright, my friend.

## Allowing Your Hinderance to Be Your Helper

The Eddie Rabbit song "Rocky Mountain Music" is a family song of ours with good memories attached. My husband was a funny man and one of the things he used to do was make up his own lyrics to songs. He would bring in names of people we knew and change the words to be funny. One time on a summer Sunday at the end of our drive home from our camper. Corey let us in on a little plan he had thought up, "Hey kids, I'm going to crank 'Rocky Mountain Music,' roll down the windows, and drive real slow past Bob's house. Let's all sing it 'Bobbie Nacho Music' real loud out the window."

It was in good fun—him trying to get a rise out of his buddy. The kids laughed as they stuck their heads out the window and yelled, "Bobbie Nacho Music fills my memory! Hehehee!" Corey sang too in a gravelly voice and then laughed, cracking himself up. I was loving it all and laughing, too. To this day, we only sing his version, and it always brings a smile. Ironically, it also brought insight to me months into my grief journey. As it was playing one day at our house, bringing up a good memory of Corey, there was one part that stuck out to me. The words grabbed my attention almost as if a messenger was giving me an anthem for me to be aware of in how I was with my kids in the wake of grief. The words went, "Momma, she got sick and mean, sometimes I think she just got that way missin' poppa."[3]

In those words, I could hear both truth and possibility—truth in how I had moments of feeling sick and tired and was missing Corey deeply. I also heard possibility in how that could become a fixed state of being. I experienced a warning: that was *not* what I wanted for my kids or myself. Yikes. Feeling ill with grief and growing mean in it was definitely a toxin daring to hinder me. But in becoming aware of myself being a hinderance to my kids, it actually empowered me. This awareness shone the light of consciousness on a dark corner, giving me the opportunity to shift, and making the toxin instead a medicine for self-change and for a change in my relationship with my kids.

Any experience that shakes up your world and leaves trauma and pain is a surefire way to turn a person sick and mean. In my experience I can feel the jadedness that has shown up in the wake of closing down due to the trauma of losing Corey. Such an experience that shatters you and changes things forever no doubt weighs-in heavy to change *you* forever. I am sharp in certain actions, thoughts, and behaviors where I never used to be. It is sometimes

---

[3] The real lyric is "sick and lean," which I only learned recently. I always heard it as "mean," so that's the impression it made on me.

irrational, like when I see a family out together at the park and feel anger towards them. Or when I see a couple out walking and holding hands and want them to just disappear from my sight.

But it hasn't quite taken me over yet. This jadedness is still playing peek-a-boo; now you see it, now you don't. But I can feel it happening and, in my awareness of it, I am given the opportunity to change. I don't want to get sick and mean. While it is true that this is a pain I don't think I'll ever fully heal from, I don't need to allow it to grow over me like a creeping vine that chokes out the light. The two can exist at the same time: the dark choking pain of woundedness *and* the vibrant light of my soul. For myself, I notice that sometimes I can't help but be overcome with the wave of emotion that runs through me. What I have learned though is: be where you are, but own it. Don't just let the wrongs go unacknowledged. Be open with yourself and others to bring your wrongs to light so that in your moments where *you* are teachable, learning through your stuff, you too can become the teacher to those who witness you in your pain.

Bad behavior at times is an expression of pain, only discernible by reading between the lines of what is happening on the surface. A mental mantra that I sometimes use in my awareness of the pain showing up as bad behavior in my kids as they grieve for their father is: *I see your pain, but I don't have to add to it.* When I engage with this perspective, it helps me to show up gentler, which is what both my children and I need. When one child is yelling and carrying on, I could easily get irritated and be short. But instead, I pause, look at them, and see their yell as the face of grief. I know there is so much going on under the surface that they cannot put words to. Their pain is coming out of them sideways. Gentleness soothes the pain. My children need to be soothed in their pain more than they need to be scolded, but they can't rationally think this through, so I have to. I have to be the first one to change in managing my own pain so that I can help them manage theirs.

## Inner Focus, Outer Focus, and Balancing Both

Even as an adult, outbursts can become an unconscious response that takes over how you are. When absorbed in the self-focus of the inner experience, a person can start to view their life through their pain. That is scary for them and has concerning implications for our human collective. The place where inner pain persists is the place where disassociation creates more pain in people. Which then gets paid forward by those not understanding that what they are doing to others is because they are hurting. In self-awareness, you don't have to be unconscious about how your pain is hurting others. You can be open and honest with yourself, and others, and call yourself out to attempt to move up and out from where you are stuck.

Once you are in connection to yourself, you can shift your focus outward to see the steps you need to take, and the people and supports you need, to help you head in a better direction. Your outer focus does not only include the people you need to do better by, it includes the people who can help you get better. Wherever you are, in whatever challenge you are going through, there are people to support you.

For myself, I am taking the multidimensional approach and have a full team of people and practices. This helps me soften the mental and emotional edge, the physical tension held from the stress of trauma and drama, and the spiritual hole of having no good answer as to why this had to happen. My people and practices include: functional medicine doctoring, occupational therapy and physical therapy, grief counseling, craniosacral therapy, massage, AcuEnergetics® therapy, widow support groups, reaching out to friends and family, responding when friends and family reach out to me, taking time to rest, being outside, walking for exercise, meditating for inner stability, sharing openly, and being fearless to let what I feel be felt.

Little by little, with inner work and outer support, you start to feel better. The vines that were closing in on you start to be manicured back into a shape that allows for some shade but also lets the light in. And in fact, the vines themselves start to take in the light too. As you connect with and integrate these hard parts into being a part of *yourself,* now you can guide along and shape them purposefully. It's the inner and the outer in unity. I am not doing this by myself at the same time that I am doing this by myself. Only I can get through this on the inside, but it takes an army on the outside to shed light and trim up those sharp edges.

## Awareness Exercise

Time to create your dream team. If you had to put together a team of supportive people and activities right now, who or what would be on your team?

- Dream it up and write it down.
- Sometimes we need to first dream it to do it. So put a little more time into imagining how it would feel to actively engage in these ways and with these people.
- Now pick some of the things you listed to do and do them. Pick someone on your list and reach out to them.
- Once you have followed through, come back to this exercise and write about how it felt to receive this support.

## Connection Practices

In being part of the larger collective, a part of the ocean, you not only seek to steady yourself by way of others, but you have presence and ability to reach out and help others to steady themselves, too. The tide comes in, and the tide goes out. Such is life. We have all been wounded, and we have all found the means of healing some of our wounds. We have all gained wisdom and learned much, but we each still have an unlimited amount of growth potential.

Your wholeness comes not only by being witnessed *by* others but also by being a witness *to* others. You are whole in the unity of being *and* doing. Through giving of yourself to others, you complete the full circle of yin-and-yang unity. You are meant to receive and to give. Give attention, kindness, and support. Be present, honest, and trustworthy. Expand your acceptance of the inner and the outer for yourself and for others. There's a funny thing that happens as you grow to accept yourself: it gets easier to accept others. Likewise, as you grow in accepting others, it becomes easier to accept yourself. This is because acceptance is the virtue of an open heart. I first learned about the virtues of the heart from one of my life teachers Kevin Niv Farrow of AcuEnergetics®, who said, "When your heart is open, it's not just open to you or them, it's open to all." When your heart contracts and closes, you diminish your ability to be accepting. So, in your relationships keep in practice with having an open heart.

1. Check in with yourself at any given moment on if you are feeling open or closed. Whatever you are doing, and wherever you are, you can pause without anyone even noticing and ask yourself: *does my heart feel open right now?* Listen and feel if your answer is yes or no. Then ask *why?*

2. Actively look for your people. Maybe you find your people due to proximity, experience, or interest, or maybe due to being opposites in something that can bring you together in understanding. Finding your people works in two directions: to you and from you. It can start by letting someone else be *that* person to you, or it can start by you being *that* person to someone else. Maybe it is in the capacity of volunteering, outreach, or coordinating a new gathering for others. Or maybe it is in a capacity that only *your* beautiful and individual heart could ever dream up.

3. Be kind. Kindness is a medicine for the toxins of your life. If you can cultivate kindness internally, it will spill over externally and others will feel its gentleness in you. Everyone likes to be treated kindly, and it feels good to feel kindness within yourself. Just imagine

all the wrongs of the world that could be soothed or made right through kindness. Kindness is a powerful force of the human heart indeed.

> Kindness is a gift everyone can afford to give.
>
> −Unknown

# 5

# FROM CONTRACTED TO EXPANDED

## *Your Relationship with God*

As I sat in my sunroom, legs curled under me and big, black book across my lap, I found myself surprised as I read along. *Huh, this is interesting,* I thought. *I never knew these sayings came from this source.* As I read further, I started to become aware that this book contained so many of the common sayings I had been hearing my whole life. Sayings like: "by the skin of my teeth," "the blind leading the blind," "don't lose heart," "a drop in the bucket," "salt of the earth," "apple of my eye," "root of the matter," "by the sweat of your brow," "wit's end," "eat drink and be merry," and "see eye-to-eye."

I had put the book down to do a little Google research and found this list went on and on. I had lived thirty-eight years without taking the time to get to know this book—the Bible—but was taking the time to read it now. *So, all along, I have been speaking words from the Bible, and I had no idea that I was,* I thought to myself. This book had been woven into my life without me even knowing it. Yet with further reading, I found that I was just starting to scratch the surface of how deeply woven its story was within me. Now that I had started, my curiosity was piqued and my spirit touched so that I would continue coming back for more.

The fact that biblical words and phrases show up in common places stretches its wisdoms far beyond the reach of religion. And to this notion, I think to myself: *who really contains God? Nothing, and no one.* Perhaps then this really is a book for all. How mystical. As I continued to read different parts, I noticed there were truths in it that resonated with me deeply—verses that were inspiring and hopeful. I could feel the energy of the words "make my heart swell" (Isaiah 60:5). Not only encouraging me to be a better version of myself, but giving me ways to do so.

Whether or not you are a member of a religion or on the fringe of one, you too are affected by the sacred texts and the spiritual fabric of the world. Perhaps, like me, there are some beliefs you hold or sayings you speak that are rooted in a spiritual origin that you haven't realized. After all, there is something transcendental about sacred texts: they have the ability to give pieces of yourself back to you by speaking truths that your heart recognizes as its own. Their words can be a source of direction, encouragement, understanding, hope, and faith. Interestingly if you read from a variety of sacred texts, sometimes you can even find that they speak the same language or say the same thing but society focuses so much on their differences that their similarity is often missed. When sameness can be found, links are made hinting to the possibility of a shared universal connectedness.

## Awareness Exercise

In this exercise you will read from various sources about good and evil to see if you can catch a tone of similarity. Additionally, I am going to have you play a guessing game as you read them. For each verse write down which tradition you would believe it came from out of the listed options. Then on the next page as you view the correct answers pay attention to your reaction. Notice if you feel surprised or curious. Maybe there are a few that really resonate, inspiring you to take a closer look at those traditions. Perhaps there is something to be discovered from a place you haven't looked yet.

From this list write down one guess for each verse: Christian, Buddhist, Muslim, Hindu, Jewish, Sikh, Indigenous, Jain, Confucius, and Taoist.

1. "Hasten to do good; restrain your mind from evil. He who is slow in doing good, his mind delights in evil."

2. "Good and evil deeds are not equal. Repel evil with what is better; then you will see that one who was once your enemy has become your dearest friend."

3. "The noble-minded cultivate roots. When roots are secure, the Way is born."

4. "Is it not so that if you improve, it will be forgiven you? If you do not improve, however, at the entrance, sin is lying, and to you is its longing, but you can rule over it."

5. "Loose us from the yoke of the sins of our fathers and also of those which we ourselves have committed."

6. "Under Heaven all can see beauty as beauty only because there is ugliness. All can know good as good only because there is evil."

7. "Answer evil with goodness; do not fill your mind with anger."

8. "Just as you do not like misery, in the same way others also do not like it. Knowing this, you should do unto them what you want them to do unto you."

9. "Dear friends, let us love one another, because love is from God, and everyone who loves has been born of God and knows God."

10. "There are two wolves and they are always fighting. One is darkness and despair, the other light and hope. Which one wins? The one you feed."

Here they are again with their sources. Are you surprised or intrigued by any?

1. "Hasten to do good; restrain your mind from evil. He who is slow in doing good, his mind delights in evil." *Buddhist* (Dhammapada 116)

2. "Good and evil deeds are not equal. Repel evil with what is better; then you will see that one who was once your enemy has become your dearest friend." *Muslim* (Al Quran 41:34)

3. "The noble-minded cultivate roots. When roots are secure, the Way is born." *Confucius* (Analects of Confucius 1:2)

4. "Is it not so that if you improve, it will be forgiven you? If you do not improve, however, at the entrance, sin is lying, and to you is its longing, but you can rule over it." *Jewish* (Bereisheet 4:7)

5. "Loose us from the yoke of the sins of our fathers and also of those which we ourselves have committed." *Hindu* (Rig Veda 7.86.5)

6. "Under Heaven all can see beauty as beauty only because there is ugliness. All can know good as good only because there is evil." *Taoist* (Tao Te Ching, Chapter 2)

7. "Answer evil with goodness; do not fill your mind with anger." *Sikh* (Guru Grant Sahib Ang 1381, Line 19)

8. "Just as you do not like misery, in the same way others also do not like it. Knowing this, you should do unto them what you want them to do unto you." *Jain* (Mahavira, Bhagavati Aradhana, 780)

9. "Dear friends, let us love one another, because love is from God, and everyone who loves has been born of God and knows God." *Christian* (1 John 4:7)

10. "There are two wolves and they are always fighting. One is darkness and despair, the other light and hope. Which one wins? The one you feed." *Indigenous* (Cherokee Native American Legend)

## Wisdom Transcends

The mix of quotes above illustrate that wisdom is not contained in any one book alone, it transcends being exclusive to a tradition. It does not belong to any one person. It does not come from any one time or place in the world. Wisdom is expansive to depths that no human will ever fully know. Yet, at the same time, wisdom can also move through *you*, as you may have moments of being wise. All of this because wisdom, no matter the form it comes in is from one true source: God. And God can leave his fingerprint anywhere.

In general, religion is a means for us to try to understand God and be with God in heart, mind, and actions. And it's a way for God to be with us. But, beyond religion there are *also* many ways to connect to God—through life itself. God's accessibility is everywhere. For example, is not God's presence in the differing shades of sky at the end of day, the beautiful variety of eye-catching flowers in a garden, and the smile of a baby that makes your heart burst with love? How about in a moment where you receive insight to solve a problem you have been grappling with or when help seems to show up out of nowhere in a time that you most need it? What about in the majesty of the mountain or the ocean and the smallness of the grain of sand? God's touch is in everything. His presence is right in front of you, at the same time that it is hidden. You do not need to limit yourself but instead, aligning with the grand expansiveness that God is, you must hope to have eyes willing to see God everywhere and in everything.

## Time for Insight

Take some time to explore your relationship with God and write down what is in your heart.

- ○ *What is my connection to God?*

○ *What would I describe as being God's presence in my life?*

○ *What is this connection like?*

○ *How open or closed am I to other people's connection to God, whether I agree with them or not?*

○ *Do I think I am 100 percent right about God? Do I think they are 100 percent wrong?*

If you are not absolute in your opinion of you being 100 percent right, then that is actually good. It means you have *flexibility*. You need flexibility to expand. In rigidness, you contract. In rigidness, you stunt growth.

## Seeing a Bigger View

I was sitting at dinner one night talking with some women in my women's business group and they were asking me how writing was coming along. I took a deep breath and, with a slight wince on my face, said, "It is such a long process." I had been working on this book for just over a year at that point. It was getting closer to completion, but with my schooling, the kids' schedules, and re-launching Moms of Meditation (where I teach meditation online to mothers), progress was at a slow crawl. "I am hoping to release it by the end of 2021, but I'm not sure if that will actually happen." I said, as a feeling of doubt crowded over my hope.

Then one of the ladies remarked, "I can imagine it is kind of scary to put yourself out there and share your story."

I perked up a little bit in my seat and said, "I am excited to share my story and hope that it can help others with where they are in their own journey." Then I sunk down a little and said, "What I am nervous about is sharing the spiritual aspect of it." I shared further about how I had recently posted on Facebook about a meditation class and how someone asked if my meditation was Christian or Eastern. In her question I got the jest that she was looking for *"the right answer."* "It caught me off-guard," I explained. "And made me wonder if this would be what it felt like to put my book out there—having people question where I am coming from, if I am Christian or not?" Then I said, "I don't really see it that way. I kind of didn't know how to answer her question because that's just not how I think of meditation—as being religious. I think of it as just being a human practice. And that's kind of my take on spirituality too, that having a connection with God is more about being human than it is about being religious. Yes, I definitely consider myself to be Christian, but I don't limit myself there. I feel like I have many ways to connect with God."

In reflecting on this fear of being judged, I still knew I must put myself out there, despite any potential backlash. I have one set of eyes that I am afforded the sight to see with through my own personal journey, and I feel moved by God to share this unique view. Also, as someone who has learned so much through other people, I understand the value of seeing a different angle through another person's life. You too are afforded the capacity to see a bigger view by not just keeping your eyes fixed through your own sight. In taking interest in the story of another person's life view you open yourself to potentially gain from the experience of doing so.

The path that one person follows is

not the correct path for any other person.

Each of us must walk his own path to enlightenment—that is the way.

– Wu Wei, *I Ching Wisdom*

One thing that can disconnect us from God is to not see the forest for the trees. When it comes to living in alignment with God, it's not about judging which view is right or wrong, it is about seeing from your own angle *with goodness* in your heart and accepting the vastness that is God's reach, and doing this without letting your up-close-and-personal view prevent you from seeing the bigger truth that God created diversity. Diversity is a purposeful, beautiful, expression of God.

God expands as your conception of God expands. God speaks to you in a language that is multidimensional. Not a booming voice from the clouds above, but a language that can be that real when you are in touch with the unbreakable connection you have with God. God speaks to you emotionally in the feelings you have. In the sense of something feeling off in your life, and with a tug at your heart to do something, or maybe to not do something. God's mental language comes in insights and inspirations. It comes in words in books, movies, music, and sometimes the words of other people. Physically, you may know God is talking to you through signs and signals in your external world: finding a lucky penny or four-leaf clover, or seeing a rainbow. In synchronicities that you could never have dreamt up in a million years—like having the right thing show up at just the right time. Often times, these communications overlap and integrate as one experience. You might have a synchronicity and get a feeling; see a sign and have a calming knowingness; or even have a random moment of inspiration paired with a nudge to reach out to someone. God speaks to you spiritually on every level: in yourself, through others, through an experience of God himself, and through the natural world. There is no place you can go where God cannot reach you.

You also must trust this vastness for others. In seeing the vastness of the walk of life God has *you* on, you must be accepting that others are also allowed their way to God. What works for one does not work for everyone. But remember that there is One that does work for all, God. In a scenario where you are unsure about what is right and what is wrong for another person, maybe having a simple rule of thumb to go by can allow you the openness of tolerance. Perhaps the rule of thumb could be something like: *if there is no physical, emotional, or mental harm, no deceit, and no destruction of other people's property, then who am I to defend or judge?* As they say, "Let go and let God."

You don't have to be a specific religion

or follow certain beliefs

for God to believe in you.

−Akeeya

## Good and Evil

In a state of openness, one can see through individual differences and be able to connect anyway. In the opposite space of intolerance, disconnect ensues. Not tolerating differences is seen in racism, discrimination, and in political, religious, or culture wars. People who indulge these intolerances have a hard time seeing how they are not the answer to the problem but that actually they are the fuel for its fire. In such strongly held intolerance, the person's heart closes. One cannot see the wisdom of truth without an open heart.

Evil allowed into one's heart makes an adversarial energy come to life inside and threatens to push out loves capacity. In this state you can do harm to others physically, mentally, and emotionally. In the disillusionment of separating oneself from love, you close off from seeing the truth of your victim's worth as a human being. Sometimes the disconnect can be so divisive that it actually stems from the unworthiness you yourself feel. Evil looks to wound and does not want to allow itself to feel remorse in wounding. However, when evil acts have been done and the perpetrator allows remorse, that is the start to opening the heart again. No matter what we do, there is still a capacity to love in us that never leaves. It is never too late to say you are sorry and turn a new leaf in unbinding your heart.

## Time for Insight

I do not know what your capacity to do harm is, but you might. You can't leave that stone unturned in doing this work for yourself. You would be missing a big opportunity. Sometimes allowing God to reach you requires seeing the areas that you block him from, the areas that you feel too unworthy to look at in yourself. Please, if you have any inclinations of persecution or harm towards others, shine the light of your awareness into those spaces now and accept that there is a disconnect that needs your attention. Be brave to do this and know that any harm that has been caused is something that can be redeemed in you.

Answer these difficult questions for yourself:

- *Am I causing any harm?*
- *What harm is it, specifically?*
- *Why am I being harmful in this way?*
- *How can I stop doing this harm?*
- *How can tolerance play a part in stopping the harm?*

Lift yourself up now by acknowledging your bravery to go here. It is in the light now so that you can see it better. It is important not to ignore the negative in your life, just as equally important to not ignore the good. Be assured there is much more about you that is positive and know that all aspects of you are worthy of love, care, and attention. All of them. You are not alone in having the capacity for good and bad—it is part of being human.

## Disconnect Clouds Awareness

Marta was a woman in her late twenties who approached me for energy therapy. When I started to see her professionally, she was living with her boyfriend and was not working. She was on disability from a work accident that had happened three years prior, and she had not yet been able to return. Her life was not where she had imagined it would be. "I am depressed and feel helpless," she expressed, saying that she wanted to improve where she was emotionally.

I had her lie down on the therapy table and placed my hands over her body to feel her energy. I was getting a sense for where to start working with her energetic flow so that this session could relieve her from some of the emotional weight she was carrying. Her energy was very heavy. I could feel the thickness of the field surrounding her body. Her heart center and throat center felt the most stuck, so I honed in there to work.

The further we got into the session, the lighter her energy became. I could feel her centers were warm and spinning in energetic release. As the energy at her throat and heart started to shift, I began talking to her about what these centers block. When I gave her insight on how depression can be a result of blocking in the throat center, and that shame is one of the emotions that blocks the throat and keeps a person from speaking up, she broke down. "I do, I feel so ashamed. I wish that things could be different," she said.

As I kept working on her energy centers, I encouraged her to keep talking about her shame. My hands hovered just above her body to have a bio-electrical releasing effect on the energy she had been holding-in while she also verbally released it. "I feel like it's all my fault," she expressed. "Life feels so out of control." As she spoke her truth, I could feel her throat center intensify with heat and then pulse, signaling that there was more openness in its functioning than when we began. With the support of the energy healing, and her self-work of letting herself open up, her energy shifted to be more uplifted and open. She allowed herself to be seen in that moment and this freed her to see herself.

As she got off of the table, she said, "I feel lighter. The room even looks brighter." She wasn't sure what her next steps would be, but she felt clearer in knowing that the struggle she was feeling inside was not serving her, and she had hope to make some changes.

After we were finished Marta excused herself to her bathroom as the session had taken place in her home. When she came back, she had a look of shock on her face. She shared that she had just found the toilet cleaning brush she had been trying to find for weeks. "This is crazy," she said. "I had looked everywhere for it but could not find it. I even went and bought a new one."

It had been right there all along. The therapy had enabled not only her body and emotions to be clearer, but her mind as well. In coming out from the cloudiness that she had been walking around in, it became obvious what was right in front of her. I learned later that she had also been struggling with, and hiding, an addiction to pain medication. For her what originally started as a focus to relieve back pain became the nightmare of feeding the monster of addiction. She felt disconnected from herself and her life, not only because of the depression but because of the addiction. This was a wake-up call, showing her how her mental state, emotional state, and even physical substances had pulled a cloak over her eyes. Until now, she wasn't seeing what she needed: a detox and the toilet brush, both to clean her shit up. The meaningful irony not lost here, is that shit can actually be used to support new growth as fertilizer; allowing goodness to grow out of a shitty situation.

Addiction is an example of extreme disconnect. In the addiction, the person is disconnected from making self-supportive choices. The addict may have positive people, positive moments, and positive areas in their life. But because of the clouded disconnect that addiction creates, that person may not be able to see the good that is there as an olive branch with which they could pull themselves up and out.

It may be that God too is talking directly to you, in loud ways, like your body getting sick or your relationships falling apart, but you are not hearing God's warning because you are unaware. In disconnect your lack of ability to see shrouds your self-awareness in knowing that you *are* actually powerful enough to choose another way. Opening up to your need for help helps facilitate connection, and connection is what gives the strength needed to persevere, especially if you are in addiction. Addiction is one of the biggest liars out there; it cuts you away from yourself and your relationships— whether it be addiction to alcohol, drugs, food, sex, gambling, gaming, or shopping. Really, any false behaviors are a thief to your soul, perpetuating disconnect: telling lies, being a bully or a bashing-gossiper, who diminishes others to feel better about themself. All of these things diminish your spirit's illumination, dimming *you* and making it so *you* cast a shadow instead of a light.

If you are engaged in a negative behavior and are *unconscious* in it, recovery is not possible, and the potential to repeat it is likely. But if you do something negative and you are *conscious* of it, there is space for recovery to be allowed and potential for it to break as a cycle of behavior.

In truth, we all have times when the negative clouds us from seeing the positive. In these moments however, it is not God who holds us back from seeing the positive potential in a negative occurrence; He is what actually makes the positive in the negative possible. The unity is in God; in that God has the unifying power to make that which seems dualistic *all* for good.

Sometimes the idea of finding the positive can feel like such a stretch, especially when we are in the thick of things. In these moments do not forget that God's presence in *everything* makes it possible to glean some good out of *anything*.

## Openness Allows You to Grow Closer to God

Another thing to be aware of that can cloud us is attachment. Sometimes we can be so attached to how we see things that there is no room for us to see it any other way. In our firm positioning, tensions can stem off from our attachment and create barriers for our connection with others, self, and even God. And let me tell you, attachment can be sneaky. You can think you are open in your belief at the same time that you can think, "No, I don't think *they* are seeing it correctly." Openness does not mean you need to gullibly believe everything you hear, but it means that you can, and you should, use discernment without being hard-nosed. God is mysterious and things are revealed in God's time, and possibly both sides, and of the same coin.

Starting in my teenage years, I built my relationship with God off of experiences that I had, conversing through the language that God shared with me. God was real to me in feelings, in signs and synchronicities, and in the natural world—like in the stories I shared earlier about the car radio changing and about feeling the spirit of the trees and the silhouette of an angel in the starry sky. I knew He was real because I knew Him in my life and could feel His nudges. In my later twenties and early thirties, I got to amplify that connection by gaining knowledge and experience with intuition and energy as another layer was added to my connection with God. I had learned a lot and had experienced a lot, but there was one part that I didn't quite get: Jesus.

One evening, my husband and I went downstairs to the family room after putting our two-year-old son to bed. Corey sat on the end of the couch, and I sat in the adjacent love seat. We had this special time together every evening, to connect through conversation as we watched TV. He was watching the Milwaukee Brewers baseball game, which I was less interested in, so I brought up a topic we had discussed off and on since becoming parents. "I respect Christianity and value the knowledge that is there, but there are truths outside of the church, like in what I have been learning about with studying energy and spiritual connection."

Corey looked at me, wondering where this conversation was heading. We had already agreed to raise our children in the Catholic faith. He was Catholic, but I wasn't a member of any organized religion. Wanting our child to know a bigger picture, beyond religion, my heart would sometimes nudge me to revisit this topic with Corey. "I don't want our son to be taught to think that he is innately bad, or that God's love is conditional. I want him to know that God loves him all the time, because God is love and has always been love," I said.

"Well, I think that too," Corey said.

"But how?" I asked. "What about the belief that God punishes people? I think in death people probably end up punishing themselves in realizing the bad things they have done, and God just holds them in love. I am not sold on the whole judgment thing."

"I believe that God does judge," he said. "I think that God punishes people who have done bad things."

"Well, what about forgiveness?" I asked. "God forgives people who have done bad things. Isn't that the same as not punishing? It just doesn't make sense to me—the whole Jesus thing. I don't think that *a person* could have taught God how to love and forgive. God, being God, would have already had the capacity to love and forgive . . . not learn it from some human's life. I don't think that one day everyone was damned and then the next day God decided, because of Jesus, that he'd start letting people into heaven." My words were a little brash.

"Well, I think you're wrong," Corey said.

Just then, it was like the world slowed down and into our conversation interjected an audible voice outside of my head. It spoke into my ear: "Listen to him." It was quick and surprising, but I didn't react. I was very familiar with receiving spiritual words, phrases, and messages—just not ones that I could *actually* hear outside of my head. *Whoa.*

At the same time, I heard Corey continue, "I think, in Jesus's heart, He showed God another way of dealing with people. And that He loved them and that showed God to love them, too." Then Corey reminded me, "Didn't you say that you wish you would have had the knowledge when you were young that Christianity gives?"

"Yes," I agreed.

"Well, it's important to me that our kids have that knowledge," he said. "We'll get them through to eighteen; and then whatever they want to believe or do beyond that is up to them."

This I could be in agreement with, so I nodded my head and replied, "Yeah." Then, turning towards the TV, I let the conversation fade as I reflected on what had just happened. *That was kind of amazing,* I thought. I wondered if maybe it was an angel telling me to listen to what he was saying, that maybe Jesus was somehow a real part of the God I already knew so well. However, even though I was spiritually being told to listen to Corey's viewpoint, I still did not *get it* for myself.

Isn't it so true that sometimes someone can tell you something but you don't have full understanding from just being told? Sometimes you have to experience it for yourself in order to get it, in order for your eyes to be opened to seeing it for yourself. I could not see or understand Jesus beyond being a man on earth. God, on the other hand, I got. I understood and felt closely connected to God. Jesus, not so much.

Fast forward from 2009 to 2018, shortly after the New Year. I was bringing in the mail and noticed a little cardboard box addressed to me. *Hmm, I wonder what this is.* As I tried to think about what it could be, I opened the box to reveal a book titled, *Mornings with Jesus.* There was a little notecard also in the box that was a bill addressed to me to pay for having ordered it. *I didn't order this,* I thought to myself. *Weird.* And wondered, *Did somebody write my name down somewhere for this to be sent to me?*

I wanted to solve this little mystery, so I Googled the company name on the bill and got their customer service number. I called the number and a woman answered. I told her, "I got this book in the mail, *Mornings with Jesus,* along with a bill, but I didn't order it."

"You say you did not order the book, ma'am?" the rep said.

"Yeah, I have no idea why this was sent to me."

"I'm sorry, ma'am. If you did not order the book, then we will not charge you for it and you can just keep it instead of paying to send it back."

"Could someone have ordered it for me?" I asked.

"You said there was a bill, so I don't think so. Sorry for any inconvenience."

As I hung up, I held the book in my hand and looked down at it. It was pretty. The front cover had a picture of a field of daisies on it; it felt warm, sunny, and inviting. I looked at the subtitle: *Daily Encouragement for your Soul—365 Devotions.* I opened the book, curious. I had never heard of a devotional before. For each day of the year, the book gave you a verse from the Bible and a personal writing from someone's life related to the verse.

Even though I wasn't looking for the book, the book had come to me. I was feeling like this happenstance was a sign, so I took a moment to check in intuitively. Closing my eyes and centering in my heart, I asked, *God, am I supposed to read this book?* What came to me next was an image in my mind's eye through my spiritual sight. I could see Jesus in my vision. Then I could feel Him beside me. Jesus was walking next to me. I got the sense that I was supposed to walk with Him. I replied inside myself: *Okay God, I understand you want me to get to know Jesus more.* I began to read that devotional book a little each day, opening myself to this Jesus of God and allowing myself to really start to get to know Him.

## Closer and Closer You Can Become

In the spring of the same year, as I was driving home from dropping Gavin and Marin off at school, an '80s song came onto the radio—"Africa" by Toto.

"I hear drums echoing tonight

but she hears only whispers of some quiet conversation.

She's coming in, 12:30 flight

the moonlit wings reflect the stars that guide me towards salvation."

"Oh my gosh, I have to call Irene," I said out loud, in disbelief that I was hearing this song *again*. I pushed the screen on the dash of my car to make a call and dialed her number. "Oh my gosh, I just gotta share this with you" I said when she answered. "So, there is this song that I have been hearing like crazy. I heard it in the car twice yesterday, and now today I drop the kids off at school, and here it is again on the radio."

Irene is one of my closest friends, so I do not have to explain why this is a big deal—she gets where I am coming from. "So, there's this one part that keeps on sticking out to me every time I hear it," I went on. "It goes, 'Gonna take some time to do the things we never have.' I know it is a message directly to me, but I don't get what the message is? Every time I hear it, I think to myself: *doing* what *things I never have?* That is the part of the song that is the message, but I don't know what *thing* I'm supposed to take time to do."

She listened and said, "That's cool. I don't know."

"I know, me neither. Just had to share because I couldn't believe this song and this message was coming up for me again."

When I got off the phone, I thought a little more about how this was unusual for me—to not be able to read into a sign's meaning. Usually, I am pretty good at feeling into signs and deciphering God's language. But now, all I felt was that the song was for me and that someday it would make sense.

Spring turned to summer and then fall arrived. In the fall, I was invited to participate in my first-ever Bible study. This aligned with my theme of the year directed by God to get to know Jesus. While I felt like I was learning more, I still had my wall up in thinking: *how can any human teach God, who knows all?* I was trying to open my heart to Jesus, but I still felt like there had to be other truths in other religions. I did not want to be one-track-minded in my spiritual study so I was also doing research across other theologies, wanting to look at belief from every angle. This thirst for knowledge was becoming a block for me, though. When I joined the study, I could feel that I was not in the same place with accepting Jesus as the other participants. Yes, I was opening up my mind to the knowledge of Jesus, but my heart hadn't expanded yet to *experiencing* Him and *feeling* belief in Him.

One day, I finally just asked one of the women who seemed to have a solid belief in Jesus, "How did you come to be able to believe in Jesus?" I was curious to hear what she had to say. Might she have some sort of key to how I could get myself to where she was in having faith in him?

"I don't know. I just believe," she replied.

I was in absolute awe of her reply. I thought, *Wow, what a luxury to just be able to believe. I am not built that way.* My analytical brain wanted proof. It wanted clarity. But my heart felt like the truth was somehow wrapped up into all of it, across multi-views, not just in one, not just in Christianity.

I kept digging and searching, doing research online and gobbling up lots of different information about Christianity and Jesus. Some pieces started to make sense, such as accounts of apparitions of Jesus and Mother Mary appearing to people—like the young shepherd boy in Kibeho, Rwanda, and the three shepherd children of Fatima, Portugal, who saw, heard, and received spiritual messages. And I could believe about the seers in Medjugorje, Bosnia, who still to this day are receiving images and messages. With my background in energy, the etheric realm, and intuition, I could grasp the miraculous supernatural.

I also read about the image of Mother Mary that still exists today—Our Lady of Guadalupe, metaphysically appearing on a cloak made of cactus fiber to a Mexican named Juan Diego in 1531. I learned about how there had been a *host*, the bread of communion, that supernaturally turned into a literal piece of bleeding human flesh during mass in Lanciano, Italy, in the 8th century. Miraculously, it has stayed intact to the point that 1,200 years later, in the 1970s, there was a scientific study done on it. This study showed that it was not just flesh but actual cardiac tissue—as in heart tissue—as in Jesus' *bleeding heart*, the symbol of His sacrifice and suffering for our unity with Him. I also learned how the blood type sampled from the host also matched the blood type sampled from flecks of the Shroud of Turin, showing them as being both type AB, which only four percent of people have. What are the odds the blood from one is the same as the blood from the other? Both miracles converged in the scientific sign of the blood. Supernatural-meets-science was helping me to believe. It was bringing me closer to fully integrating within me, *Okay, this Jesus dude—He's for real.*

Then I stumbled upon a video about the Shroud of Turin, which is revered as the burial cloth that Jesus was wrapped in when he was put into the tomb before his resurrection. The Two Preachers 2018 *Shroud of Turin Revelations* video on YouTube[4] goes into the science of it, which is sometimes easier to grasp than the spiritual backing. One point made in the video was about how the image of Jesus's face on the shroud is a negative image, like from an old camera, when the image inverts onto the film. They also talk about how it would have taken several *billion* watts of light to superimpose the image onto the cloth. Over the five years that scientific studies were done to try to replicate the superimposed image, the amount of light needed was not reproducible—pointing to the conclusion that the means by which the Shroud of Turin was produced is not humanly possible. Supernaturally created but scientifically verified. This was a big serving of digestible information that I could process and integrate; giving proof of it being both unexplainable and believable at the same time.

Then came three powerful words. I can't remember where exactly I read this concept for the first time, but the words were: *Jesus is God.* And that's when the mic dropped. That's when all the inner struggle of trying to form my understanding of who Jesus was became clear. I thought, *If Jesus is God . . . then that explains everything.* Those simple but profound words brought it all together for me. The whole make-up of the trinity—Father, Son, and Holy Spirit—is the expression of God's multidimensionality, duality, and unity all in one.

In my ongoing and developing relationship with God, I had spent many years not seeing what I didn't have the eyes to see in knowing Jesus. At the

---

4 You can watch this video at https://www.youtube.com/watch?v=fWH9o_fUpXl

same time, I was open to seeing a lot with the eyes I did have to see with, the eyes of supernatural sight and the subtle senses of feeling energy. Both the seeing and the not seeing shaped me, so that in God's time I got to open up to what I didn't already see. By following God's nudges, my own inner inclinations, and learning through others, I was able to, as the song goes, "take some time to do the things [I] never have" and connect with Jesus. I am sure God's unfolding is not done yet, and there is even more to come. What I have come to know is that it all was of God: the order, the depth, the unfolding. But this is not unique to me; it is happening in your life, too. Your experiences and openings may look different, but the same is true for you. Your life is giving you an opportunity to grow closer and closer to God.

For the grace of God has been revealed,

bringing salvation to all people.

−Titus 2:11

## What Is God's Story?

These are just my breadcrumbs, my story, and my journey. It is just one version of how expansiveness-in-God allows one to open more *vs.* being contracted. In contraction, the closedness can keep a person stalled and disconnected from the changing life experience that *is* in connection with God.

I have found that I do enjoy the different dimension of closeness to God that is available in Christ. And I wonder, what if it is possible that God *does* have one grand story, and what if it is also true that God *does not* have just one story? Couldn't both be true? God's one story is His story, and God's many stories are ours. Can you believe your life is God's story, too?

Have a think on this: same question, different answers:

Can we ever really know God? Nope.

But can we ever really know God? Yes.

*Nope,* in that you can never know God because He is too big for us to know. This is held in the many stories of God—that is His great mystery. And *yes,* because you can know God personally. The One story of God is for us to know Him. God's story is like the yin-yang. In it being *both* yes and no, these equally true answers express duality in their difference but have the same one answer in God. To one degree, you can never know God in His mystery. At the same time, you can very closely know God in His mystery. The One is in the many, and the many are in the One. And the whole of both is God.

A friend once shared this story. A Christian and a Buddhist were having a conversation. The Buddhist said: "Do you know what your problem is? All you Christians think you need Jesus to save you."

To which the Christian replied, "Do you know what your problem is? All you Buddhists think you can save yourself."

They were both right. Both right in varying degrees. Isn't that what life is made up of varying degrees that differentiate you from me and varying degrees that make us the same? We can't save ourselves alone, nor does believing in Jesus save us from ourselves. Also, at the same time you need God to save you and you need to save yourself, too. We are co-creators with God in a divine mix of destiny and free will. So, there are varying degrees to how some of it shows up in your story. It's like the Eric Church song "Some of It":

"Some of it you learn the hard way.

Some of it you read on a page.

Some of it comes from heartbreak.

Most of it comes with age.

And none of it ever comes easy.

A bunch of it you maybe can't use.

I know I don't probably know what I think I do,

But there's somethin' to,

Some of it."

The 'some of it' is wisdom. There are many ways to live and many ways to learn. Sometimes you get it right and sometimes you don't. And sometimes you live through the wrong in your life, with God's breadcrumbs leading you along in your unfolding journey. God meets you where you are and nudges you to where He would like to see you go. Listen to and trust God's nudges for you because there's something to, 'some of it.'

## Your Relationship with God

Anytime a person is stuck in a belief system that pits them against other living, breathing human beings, they aren't picking up what God is putting down. Every human has a right to have their own beliefs without persecution. Yet it can happen in religion that people get so closed-minded that they believe *their* way is God's way and take license to judge, persecute, or attack others. This is true disconnect: when your heart has left God's building of being in sync with God's love for all.

This is a scenario, which can happen in any religion, in which the religion becomes more of a hinderance than a help, more of a toxin then a medicine. But it often comes more from how a person is in the religion than from the real teaching of it. Religion is man-made, so it is not perfect. But spirituality is God-made, and placed innately in you. In all of us.

Your spirituality, not your religion, is your most direct connection to God. God meets us, wherever we are, in our hearts. Your true relationship with God comes from inside of you. That is the closest place you can know God and be with God—through your innate, inner connection with Him. God is as close as the beat of your heart and as far away as the stars in the sky. No matter what your perception of your connection with God is—near, far, or non-existent—you are still in relationship with God because God is the source and perpetual mover of your life.

Being in relationship with God involves reciprocation. Like any relationship, there is a two-way sharing of language that calls for an openness to listen, and a willingness to share and dialogue. Both listening and speaking with God to connect is to commune with God. You're not going to get a reply to your heart's question if you never ask it. And you're not going to hear the reply if your heart isn't open to receive it.

## Connection Practices

One practice that can be used to explore your connection with God is in doing an active type of meditation in which your intention is to openly dialogue. In general, meditation creates a space to sit in open awareness. It readies the soil of the soul and welcomes God's planting of communication in your life. Begin by spending time first in the stillness of being in meditation. When the steadiness has come and the openness is ripe, talk to God and listen for what reply does come. It might be instant. It might be delayed. It might be hours later in a sign, a word, or a song. It might be what you expect or it might not be what you were hoping for. It's okay to ask again and again and to ask for clarification. Remember that the heart can hear God best. As in any relationship, connection builds over time and the language builds with practice.

1. Sitting with God:
   - Find a quiet place where you will not be interrupted.
   - Open with the meditation of just feeling your breath. Sit in just *being*.
   - Then shift to an active meditation of *doing* by asking God a question. It could be something like, *God what is something you want me to focus on in my life?*
   - After asking your question, just notice what you notice. Pay attention to if there is anything you feel you are receiving as a reply. Wait with openness for God's language and timing to show up in response. Remember, it might or might not be immediate.

2. Get curious through openness. Seek deeper knowledge in an area of familiarity or seek fresh knowledge in an area of the unknown. Read a book, listen to a podcast, or watch a video that shares a perspective to contemplate spirituality and God's diversity.

But most importantly, watch for God's personal nudges as to where he wants you to explore. Pay attention to the things that seem to pop-up randomly. He will direct you best to where you should be connecting.

3. Prayer. Prayer is just openly talking to God. It is similar to the meditation practice above, except that it's more one-sided in that you are petitioning to him for what you feel is needed in your life or others' lives. I used to think prayer was something only religious people did. That was a big misperception on my part. Once I got involved with my circle of intuitive friends and I saw from their example that you can just simply talk to God as prayer, it made more sense to me and I started to use prayer to connect and communicate. What is simpler than going to the person you want to communicate with and saying what is on your mind? You can talk to God at any time, in any way. Start with, "Hey, God," and then let your heart take it from there. No need to complicate the uncomplicated—it is just talking.

When you give to God your time and attention, God will certainly give back to you. Don't be too busy for God. Don't miss reaching out to the source that is always there for you. In doing so you would be cutting yourself off from the loving flow of your life's spring.

Look beyond what you know, know what you look beyond to…

God is uncontained…

and so are the many avenues to which we can reach Him

and to which He can reach us.

Be open to the season of change and allow your heart to be changed

in the discovery of something new, in Him.

# 6

# FROM HEAVEN TO EARTH

## *Your Relationship with Earth*

My mom tucked me in to bed, covering me with the multi-colored afghan-square blanket that Grandma Slanker had recently finished crocheting for me. It was special, and I felt special. I smiled to myself and pulled it up, clinging it lovingly to my chest. Mom walked to the bedroom door and turned off the light. She stepped out of the room, looking back in to say, "Night-night, love you, see you in the morning."

"Night-night," I said back. She smiled at me and then walked away leaving the door open a smidge. It was only 8:30 p.m., and my seven-year-old self was not feeling tired. I laid in the dark and looked around my room. I noticed that the colors on my toys, my rug, and the wall were muted in gray. A light from a car passing by outside shone on the wall. I watched the beam of light as it moved from left to right, as if driving through my room, and disappearing. I rolled over and my eyes were drawn upwards to the window beside the bed. I looked out, picked the first star I saw, and recited in a whisper, "Star light, star bright, first star I see tonight. I wish I may, I wish I might, have this wish I wish tonight." Sending a little message out to that star to hear my heart's desire. While all the other stars sparkled in the sky like shiny freckles on the face of the universe.

After a while, I sat up and stretched my neck to peer out my window, curious if the moon was out. There she was. I spotted her to my left, just coming up over the blooming white cherry tree whose big branches were like thick arms of a spider in my backyard. I stared at her glow, and then looked out across our family farm's sod field just beyond the yard. I noticed how the moon cast light in all directions and made it seem like daytime at night. The cattails in the ditch seemed to wink at me as they rustled in and out of the moon's reach. From dark to light, I could see them change. My eyes were drawn back up to the glittering sky. I noticed the smoky chain of the Milky Way and two big stars that seemed to shine brighter. *I wonder how far away they are?* I thought. In my mind, I measured from myself to the moon and then beyond to the stars. *Wow, how far does out there go?* I wondered. I lay back down, closed my eyes, and allowed myself to drift off to the other magical space of my dreams.

In gazing at the night sky as a child, my heart was captured. The stars and the moon imparted a gentle peace in my heart. My sister Lynnette once told me that when I was really little, I would point up into the night sky and say, "That's my star." There was an identity, a connectedness, an ownership of it being for me and of me. In the innocent awareness of a little girl, there was a subliminal knowingness of connection. We all have a wisdom stored inside of us that speaks to our connectedness. We all come from the same thing—of heaven and of earth. We all come from what the stars are made of. We are cosmic in nature, in spirit, and in beauty.

The nitrogen in our DNA, the calcium in our teeth, the iron in our blood,

the carbon in our apple pies were made in the interiors of collapsing stars.

We are made of starstuff.

–Carl Sagan, *Cosmos*

Our bodies are made of the burned-out embers of stars that were released

into the galaxy in massive explosions billions of years ago,

mixed with atoms that formed only recently...

All of that is not just remote history but part of us now:

our human body is inseparable from nature all around us

and intertwined with the history of the universe.

—Karel and Iris Schrijver, *Living with the Stars*


The natural world is a miracle. You are a miracle of the natural world. As you are made of star dust, you most certainly carry a twinkling of the universe inside your body and your soul. There is a dimension of the universe that is physical, that is substance, but there is also the dimension that is spiritual, or non-physical. The language of the natural world is not only in the physical building blocks of life deciphering what the details of an organism are but it is also in the essence of life. Life force is dispersed across the many expressive creations of earth. As the inanimate is enlivened through the animate, earth is blessed to come alive. A purposeful mix of dualism explained in Traditional Chinese Medicine is that heaven is considered to be yang and the earth is considered to be yin. Yang moves through yin forms to animate them. Yin is the vessel through which the heavenly yang can move. Heaven and earth as one create this world of perpetual form and motion.

## Interconnection of Heaven and Earth

As a college student at Grand Valley State University, I had left my small town and was in the next phase of growing up. Despite everything being unfamiliar, this transition was easy. I was ready to stand on my own. Feeling settled with the new flow of life, I ventured out with college friends one day to the bigger city of Grand Rapids to see a movie. We chose to see *Stigmata*, a thriller about an atheist who supernaturally suffers the wounds of Christ. At the time, I was more interested that it was a horror film and did not know what stigmata was. We sat in the top row, sipping Coke and eating popcorn as the film rolled. It was interesting and creepy, so my attention was hooked. Then words were spoken in the film that felt like they were being spoken personally to me. "Jesus said . . . the Kingdom of God is inside you, and all around you, not in mansions of wood and stone. Split a piece of wood . . . and I am there, lift a stone . . . and you will find me." This line in the film spoke to God being everywhere and in everything: in nature, in me. The words reached out to me as if God was saying, *I see you and you see me.*

*Whoa, that's what I believe,* I thought. It was a quote from the Gospel of Thomas in the Dead Sea Scrolls. As the movie went on, I sat there a bit stunned. In that moment, those words felt like they were from God's mouth directly to me. I had felt connected to God through nature for many years, but I had never come across anything before that had reflected this back to me. To have the words so blatantly spelled out made a lasting and solidifying impression. Not only are you not separate from the natural world, but God is not separate from it. Earth is a supreme connector of infinite proportion. It is where you and God connect.

## Heaven Speaks through Earth

From the day that Corey asked me to marry him to the day we got married on the beach in Marco Island, Florida, I made it a point to talk to my mom more often. She had passed away three years prior, but I still needed her. I needed to know she would be with us. "Mom, I want you to show me that you are with us on our wedding day by sending us a beautiful sunset," I told her. She heard this from me many, many times as I kept hoping my wish would come true.

On the day of our wedding, we gathered on the beach just before sunset with our immediate families. The nerves of the day were calmed in seeing each other and knowing that this was it—in a good way. My heart swelled as I held Corey's hands and looked up into his gentle, loving, green eyes.

The wedding officiant said, "Now we'd like to take a moment to remember those who cannot be here with us in body today." I bowed my head and connected inward, thinking of my mom and bringing her into the moment within me. Next came our beautiful ceremony and the joy of being joined in the union of marriage. Afterwards, the photographer began organizing our group for photos on the beach. The sun was going down, but we weren't getting any color. Due to it being a bit cloudy, the sky was a mix of gentle shades of blue and gray. Because of the lackluster sky, the photographer was also taking some pictures with the tall buildings behind us to create a picturesque scene. It did not appear we were going to have the colored sunset I had hoped for. But then, as we were being positioned, I had a moment to look out across the water to the sky and think of Mom. I spoke to her again in my heart, looking for her to bring herself into the moment and show up for me.

I thought to myself, *Okay, Mom, where's your big thing?* A split second later, the sky *erupted*: yellow, gold, blue, pink, orange, and violet colors magnificently splayed across the sky. They were colors of love and light replying back to me: *I am here. I am here.* I had never before seen a sunset so vibrant and beautiful. It was by far the best wedding gift Corey and I could have received—right from heaven.

In my life, I have been gifted with some profound communications received through the natural world, another of which involved my dear Corey. After Corey died, we could not have his funeral for four months due to COVID-19 restrictions, so I had a chance to put a request in with him in heaven, too. *Corey, send us a rainbow on the day of your funeral,* I asked.

The time finally approached and, with mixed feelings of honor and despair, our children, Corey's parents, and I began to celebrate his life. We held a visitation at the church the evening before his funeral where we invited people to come pay respects and give condolences. Face-to-face human contact is so important at times like this. My two best friends from high school, Maxine and Fran, also flew in to be with me. The day was busy and I hadn't had much of a chance to sit with them, so I asked my family if they could take the kids so that I could stop for a quick bite with my friends. That worked for everyone. I finished up what was needed of me at the church and left to meet them.

Restaurants were still restricted and some were even still closed, so we planned to go to a drive-thru and eat outside. As I was waiting to place my order, I looked out of the open window of the car into the sky and gasped. "Oh my gosh, Corey!" I said out loud as I saw a big, beautiful rainbow arching through the sky. It hadn't even been raining. What a miracle. I quickly grabbed my phone and took a bunch of pictures. As I continued through the line, I watched the rainbow, not wanting to take my eyes off of it —off of his love. Then it gently faded away, its colors melting back into the sky. Later that evening, my dad, and his wife Lee Ann also saw a rainbow. And the next day, my sister Lynnette, brother-in law Rob, and niece Samantha saw one, too. The colors of Corey's love were able to reach through the ethers so that we could know he was with us. He still sends us rainbows from time to time. He also comes to us in music, hawks and eagles, and in lucky pennies—earthly things endowed with heavenly energy. Showing that the connection with those we love is unbreakable in the face of any earthly changes we may go through.

Because spirit is intimately intertwined with the earth, spirit can speak through the natural world. In every natural thing, spirit is speaking. Sometimes the speaking is just the flow of life. But sometimes the speaking is directly to you.

## Your Connection to the Earth

Because you are earth on the inside and the world is earth on the outside, there is a continuity of energy between you and your surrounding world. If we could take away the lines of form that separate, we would see a continuous life force filling in the space of earthly matter. This connectivity is why we can feel the energy of nature. When I watch birds flying, I feel their movement in my body as a mirrored sensation. As the bird's wings flap up and down, I feel that movement of up and down inside my body. It's as if to say, we are one. Also, we are not able to look directly at the sun, it is too powerful for our eyes, but when I look at a photograph of the sun's rays shining through, I can feel the sun's powerful energy soothing my spirit. Somehow the energy of the sun has been captured in the photo in such a way that I can feel its radiant light.

My kids have also noticed at times how they can feel nature. Once while walking through the forest, my kids and I came upon a large cottonwood tree. We guessed it to be a few hundred years old. As we got closer, the energy around us shifted in a subtle way. There was a vibrational change entering the energy field of the tree and we could feel this. Its grand energy emitted a heart-centering, grounding, and tangible presence that we could feel mellowing us out. The trees energy was connecting with our own energy, making our hearts feel peaceful.

"Can you feel that?" my son asked.

"The energy of that tree, yes," I confirmed. "What does it feel like to you?"

He shared how he was feeling tingly and peaceful. "It feels good," he said. He too could feel the big energy of the tree within his own body. We stood there together, eyes closed to focus on the energy, both noticing how good it felt.

## Awareness Exercise

You too can build up ability for feeling the spirit of nature. You can hear its subtlety just like you hear everything else—by listening. In this case, with all of your senses: the physical and the non-physical. Listening with complete awareness that spans the inside and outside of you. The following is a simple practice you can do to amplify your senses and build your ability. The natural world is a great healer, so it is worth your time to learn how to take in its energy in a heightened state of awareness.

o   Take the time now to go outside or to a window.

o   Get comfortable in whatever position is relaxing for you.

o   Take five minutes to be an open observer of the natural world. Allow it to be unscripted as you focus outward, letting your senses absorb the natural world.

o   Reflect on the experience. Maybe you were able to watch a bird or look at the clouds. Maybe you watched a tree sway in the wind or noticed the vibrancy of the colors around you. Maybe you felt something in yourself; an opening.

o   Now, go back to looking around you while outside or through your window.

o   This time, as you open your senses to nature, ask yourself, "How does this make me feel? How does stopping and connecting with nature make me feel?"

o   If you like, write down these observations.

There is peace available to you when you slow down and connect to nature with your open awareness. The natural world is soothing to your emotions, gentle to your mind, stilling to your body, and uplifting to your spirit. Earth is a wealth of nurturing energy that, when tapped into, can wash through all dimensions of your being—nourishing mind, body, emotion, and soul. Nature is innately healing. Her lush greens cascade into your energy field as healing, her moving waters flow through your energy as cleansing, her rays of light charge you so you may feel illuminated. Not only are these the life-sustaining building blocks of your body— in water, food, and light energy —but they are the reparative frequencies of emotion, body, and mind. The healing potential of the earth substance and essence are a natural part of our world.

## Connecting with Nature to Soothe

"Mom, this milk tastes funny," six-year-old Gavin said as two-year-old Marin whined at me from the table.

"Hang on, Marin. Yours is coming," I said as the toaster popped. She was growing impatient waiting for her breakfast.

"Mom, this doesn't taste good," Gavin said again.

"Gavin, I heard you. You're going to have to wait a minute," I said impatiently as I finished spreading strawberry jelly on Marin's toast.

"Marin, that's mine!" Gavin yelled.

I turned around to see Marin had scooted herself up onto the table on her belly and was pulling apart the Lego pieces Gavin had saved for later building.

"Marin, get down," I hollered.

Gavin got up and roughly grabbed his Legos from her chubby little toddler hands.

"Gavin, be gentle," I warned, bringing Marin's jelly toast and vanilla yogurt to the table. She was on her belly, her legs dangling off the side of the table. I picked her up and sat her down on her butt. "Okay, eat, Marin."

"I'm hungry," Gavin reminded me. I grabbed Gavin's bowl and headed over to the counter. Picking up the carton of milk and looking at the date, I sighed. The expiration date was a week ago. I opened up the carton, took a sniff and, sure enough, it was sour.

I went to dump it down the kitchen sink when Gavin grumbled, "I want cereal."

I heard Marin chime in, "Spooooon," and looked over to see her attempting to eat her yogurt with her fingers.

"The milk is spoiled, Gavin. Do you want jelly toast?" I said, as I looked for a toddler spoon.

"I don't want jelly toast," he said as I opened the dishwasher. Everything was dirty.

"Spooooon," Marin repeated, moving her yogurt-covered fingers to her mouth.

"Mom, what can I have?" Gavin asked with frustration.

"What do you want, Gavin?" I said irritated, not wanting to have to list out options like a menu. I began to wash off the toddler spoon.

"I don't know. What can I have, Mom?" Gavin said.

"How about fruit and yogurt?"

"Okay," he decided.

I went over to Marin who was on her tummy and hanging off the chair now. I put the spoon in her yogurt, picked her up, and sat her back on her butt.

"Sit down and eat," I told her sternly. I quickly spooned some yogurt onto a plate for Gavin and added cubed muskmelon from the fridge. "Here," I said, as I placed the plate in front of him.

"I want my yogurt in a bowl," he said.

"Gavin, eat the yogurt," I told him. "I am not going to get you anything else."

Just then, Marin started crying. She had toppled out of the chair and onto the ground. I picked her up again and sat her back down.

"If you would just sit down, you wouldn't fall off the chair," I said. She continued to cry as I handed her spoon to her again, encouraging her to keep eating. She threw her spoon down.

"No!" she yelled.

"Fine," I said gruffly, as I grabbed a rag to wipe off her jelly-and-yogurt-covered face and hands. Then I heard a crash on the floor. Gavin had bumped Marin's bowl of yogurt and it had fallen upside down onto the floor. "Ugh, Gavin! What are you doing?" I yelled. My head was spinning and my anger was in my throat, lashing out like the tongue of a snake. Emotion was bleeding into a discharge of energy that could no longer be contained in my small frame. I knew this was not a good start to the day for any of us. So, I tried to turn my back on all of it. I quickly wiped up the spilled yogurt with the rag and declared, "We need to go outside."

Within moments of going into the backyard, all three of us settled down. I slowly walked across the green grass, giving myself space from the kids as they sped over to the playset. Gavin climbed onto the swing and Marin toddled up her plastic slide. Our spirits were uplifted just by being outside. With no walls to dull the vibrations of nature or block our senses to her,

Earth[5] soothed us and gave us space to be. No one was fighting anymore. In fact, the kids were now content and happy. Still holding onto the residual feeling of defeat, I lingered and sat down in the soft grass, taking a moment for myself. With nothing pressing on my energy or my psyche, I had enough space to stop and breathe. And so that's all I did—just breathed and took notice as I looked across my yard at the green grass and trees. I absorbed the gentle vibration of the greenery and was soothed. I noticed the energizing rays of golden sun as they warmed the top of my head. I felt the coolness of the breeze move through my hair. I even zeroed in on the buzz of a cicada from somewhere in the trees and was able to take in its melody as a means of soothing my being. Our mothering Earth wrapped her healing arms around me, calming my emotions, soothing the tension of my frazzled edges, and resetting me mentally in the respite of her beauty observed. Connecting me to my soul through the breath she breathed into me, I felt lulled from the inside and out, from the combined energy of both spirit and earth, one in wholeness.

It requires only a pause and a listening heart to allow yourself to be soothed in nature's presence. Your connection with nature is un-detachable. You are always linked into her because she is a life source for all of humanity. She is humanity's home, and she is the cosmic womb that birthed us. Though she never fails you, at times, you fail yourself by not tapping into the plentiful resource of her soothing presence. She is there for you, ready to hold you, if you pause long enough to let her.

### Earth's Multidimensions

The earth itself is another expression of unity, duality, and multidimensionality. The unity of the earth is that it is but one place. Our only home in the universe. Humans are dependent solely on the earth.

Then there is the duality that plays out on earth: day and night, dark and light, birth and death, growth and decay, east and west, young and old, hot

---

[5] Earth is capitalized to denote Earth's presence as a being.

and cold, up and down, left and right, dim and bright, broken and fixed, lost and found, silence and sound, soft and hard, small and large. And the list goes on.

And multidimensionally, the earth has many expressive variations in its form and movement. The differing forms of land, water, air, and light are synonymous with the four elements of earth, water, air, and fire that form the constructs of our world. Then there is planetary movement in the collective momentum of the earth revolving around the sun and rotating in space. There is also movement in the elements, in the natural world, by means of destruction and creation. The four elements are in relationship with one another and their interaction causes change. For example, water to earth can be nourishing, as in quenching rain to crops, but it can also be destructive, like floods destroying those same crops. There is even movement in the human collective as a whole: we are all spinning forward on earth together in time and space. Each of us is affected by global changes like natural resource depletion, climate change, agricultural and technological advances, changes in medicine and health, and global political structures. There is also momentum in the shifting patterns of the collectives in our world—via groupings of people sharing similar ideas, actions, and practices. Then there is the movement of each individual, who has an intricate intertwining of personal and impersonal connections to all of the movement going on in the multidimensions of the world. Movement of life is like a river, constantly in motion; and God the sea we all are flowing to.

"The river is flowing, flowing and growing,

The river is flowing back to the sea,

Mother Earth is carrying me her child I will always be,

Mother Earth carry me back to the sea."

–Native American folk song, "The River is Flowing"

## Time for Insight

Even though you live immersed in an experience that feels personal, you are not separate from that which is impersonal and feels further from you. The personal and impersonal are connected. Not only do you leave a fingerprint on your life, but you leave a footprint on the earth. Not only do you affect those around you, but you affect the larger collective that is humanity. This effect is a dimension of the oneness on earth. We have a symbiotic relationship with Earth as a being; the summation of the impressions we leave either contribute to or detract from its greater good. There is a momentum that you are a part of, adding weight to the scale of which direction the world is heading in. Take a moment now to write your answers to these questions in order to gauge where you are in your relationship with Earth.

- *Am I leaving an imprint that adds to or takes away from the earth?*
- *Am I adding to chaos or adding to peace regarding the state of the earth?*
- *Do I think that the collective direction of humanity is moving towards unity inside earth's duality? Why?*
- *Do I think that the collective direction of humanity is moving towards destruction because duality is functioning outside of its unity? Why?*
- *Which direction do I think is currently stronger?*
- *Which direction do I want to see be stronger?*
- *What can I do in my relationship with the earth to strengthen moving in that direction?*

## Caring for the Earth

On a sunny spring morning, near the end of the kids' school year, I was at Como Zoo, chaperoning Marin's first-grade field trip. I was walking along behind the girls, following their lead. First, they wanted to walk through the reptile house to reach the orangutans. Next, we were on our way to see the giraffes. A baby giraffe had recently been born, so this was a highlight to visit.

As we walked, I noticed that Marin and her classmate were having such a good time. The zoo had created a wonderful space for people to grow a greater appreciation for the animals. They were also educating visitors by sharing important and interesting facts about the animals. It was obvious that the people who took care of the zoo did so with pride, caring not only for the animals, but keeping the landscape and the walkways clean and beautiful so that it could be enjoyed by everyone.

The girls and I were passing by a snack shack, nearing the giraffe area, when I saw a young woman in front of me walking with a bag of chips. She finished her last bite from the bag, put her arm down by her side, and dropped the bag on the ground. I kept watching, expecting that she would pick it up. But she just kept walking. I was in disbelief. She didn't look down, she didn't look around her, she didn't appear to have any regard for what she had just done. *What the heck,* I thought to myself. She had been just ten steps from a garbage can when she dropped the bag. I couldn't understand her behavior and it disgusted me. It was blatant disregard for the earth, the zoo, and the people around her. I wanted to say to her, *Clean up after yourself, lady!* But instead, I picked up the empty bag of chips and threw it away. Sometimes our efforts are able to reverse the ill effects that a disconnect in another person created. Sometimes our efforts are not only needed but necessary.

Stewardship is one obvious area where we can all make a positive impact in caring for the physical world. We each have a responsibility to care for our earth because it is a relationship like any other and thus operates through reciprocation. It is not a one-way street. Put simply: you should care for the Earth because she cares for you. Everything you need to live is provided for by her. You cannot get what she gives you in any other place in the universe. She is special, beautiful, and worthy of your care and attention. Caring for her allows her to be better able to care for you and others. Build your connectivity to Earth in *appreciation, respect, and responsibility,* and see where that takes you and what impact you can make.

Earth is a being, a place, a collective of mixed cultures, and is beautifully breathtaking when seen with open eyes. Yet, with closed hearts, one does not see her beauty at all. Too self-absorbed to notice. The self-absorption of a closed heart is disconnection, and when there is a lack of connection to Earth, your connection to God, to others, and to yourself is weakened.

Caring for earth is also caring for the present people, the future children, and generations to come. It is about not only preserving life but about leaving a legacy for a good life—even a better life. This is a widely held idea, but is it a widely held *feeling*? An idea is of the mind, but a feeling is of the heart. When the heart is connected, there is more understanding and motivation for what actions are needed for the relationship to be felt, not just thought about. Not only is spending time in nature going to benefit you, but it will help build your appreciation of the natural world to take responsibility for its care for the sake of yourself and others and with reverence for God's creation.

My relationship with Earth is personally the one I feel the least connected to these days out of the four. Life seems so automatic: the sun always shines; day and night always follow each other. Water always flows from the tap and the breeze always blows through the open window. Anything that is constant and reliable can so easily be taken for granted. I have found that it helps me to stay connected by practicing mindful consideration of the nature around me. You too can be mindful to do things like take the time to pick up garbage that you see in your neighborhood. Take the time to upkeep your own yard, garden, or community space. Buy a bird feeder and leave out food. You might even discover that you feel joy in watching the birds while caring for nature. It is a healthy indicator that you have a connected relationship with Earth when you can feel grateful for her bounty, and that your needs are met, by reciprocating looking out for Earth's needs too.

## You Are Earth

When you are disconnected from the earth, you also set yourself up to be missing insight and connection that you could be getting about yourself. The language of the earth gives you a perceptive window into yourself. It reflects back to you because, earth to reader, *you are earth*. The whole is contained in the part and the part is contained in the whole.

You are an extension of Earth, so with the right eyes you can see yourself reflected in her. Earth is expressive of us. She tells a story that tells you about yourself and, when you listen, you can hear yourself in the echoes of creation amplified through her. For example, the patterns of weather are like your ever-changing emotions. Some days are sunny and happy, some gloomy and sad, and others stormy and angry. Some conditions are harsh and others lush and comforting. The seasons mirror change, too. As one season ends and another begins, some things in life sprout while others die away. There are seasons to your life.

Another example is how the inside of the lungs are shaped like the branches of trees. We have internal lungs, but the trees are our external lungs. Both make breathing possible. The earth's water system is that the rain comes down from above to nourish life and vegetation. Your inner water system is also like rain coming down through you—as you drink, hydration is distributed through you and nourishes your cells. And the rivers moving through the land are like the veins carrying blood through your body.

You resemble Earth, and the Earth resembles you. You are one body with many cells. The Earth is one body with many people. Each cell and each person have their own function and life span that rolls into the continual creation of new cells and new people. Thus, the body's balance and the earth's balance are sustained. In this echoing of life, you can be spoken to through the things that make up the earth, as they explain aspects of yourself. Here is a piece of my writing that lends another illustration of this:

## You Are a Diamond

A diamond is created under pressure.

Remember this when life is at its peak of challenge,

that you are just creating your diamond through it.

On the way to bursting with your inner light, and crystallizing with clarity,

you discover you are stronger than that which pushes hard against you.

More beautiful and more unbreakable than at the start.

Internal evolution is the way of the diamond, and pressure, its catalyst.

## Health Is Earth's Wealth

Your connection to the earth is symbolic and figurative, but it is also literal. Another dimension of our relationship with the earth is through our food. Light given from the sun—solar energy—is taken in through your skin, affecting mood and chemistry, such as vitamin D levels. Sunlight is also taken in by plants and stored in their cells. When we ingest those plants, this light energy transfers into our systems. Earth communicates as food, speaking to the cells of your body. When the food is nutrient-dense and high quality, it fuels cells optimally and supports their function and health. When the food lacks nutritional value, cells do not get the fuel they need and this leads to a decline in health. When you have a disconnect with what you put into your body and consume unhealthy things, it ends up having an effect not only on you physically, but mentally, emotionally, and energetically.

It is helpful to have an awareness for connecting with your body in regards to the substances you put in because your body being the extension of earth that it is, also is earth to care for. Just like you must pay attention to when garbage in your external environment needs to get cleaned up, you too need to be mindful of when to clean up your internal environment. You have to figure out what best supports your body's vibrance. In exploring this it is important to listen and pay attention to what your body says back to you on the matter.

I am certain that one of my life lessons is to learn how to *be friends* with my body. I think a lot of us have this lesson to learn, as self-acceptance and body image can be such an intertwined beast. Currently, I am working with my body to support a reversal of the low energy and brain fog that has crept in over the last several years. I have been both eliminating and adding different combinations of things to find a steady balance for optimal functioning. The language my body and I have mostly been communicating in—is food.

Food *is* medicine, but it can also be a toxin when you eat the wrong things for your body. Anyone, who has a food allergy is testament to this. Food's potential to be a help or a hinder in some cases is dependent on the quality of food or quantity of food, and in other cases is dependent on your body's tolerance. In being a student of my body, I have been fascinated to learn that certain foods give me a food hangover—increased tiredness, irritability, and lowered mental function show up and then take time to wear off. Sometimes the wearing off of the ill effect can take several weeks. Yuck, right? Yet, I don't always stay away from these foods due to darn temptation, but when I do, I feel better. In taking the time to eliminate things and then add them back in experimentally, I have built a greater awareness of when I am having food-specific backlashes. This self-knowledge gives me more motivation to stay on track with what works best for my body. Even though it can seem like a constant work in progress—sometimes getting up and out of a food spiral and sometimes falling back into one—no matter where you are in your patterned behavior with food it is worth being conscious about to support your needs.

Your body is not to be disregarded or ignored but listened to. The earth has an operating intelligence and your body has this same intelligence. The body can wisely tell you what you need when you are attentive to its language. It takes seeking knowledge to learn your options, experimentation to gather data to get a clearer picture, and experience to back up the data: *if I do this I feel like garbage* and *if I do this, I feel like a million bucks.* It is important to notice the different dimensions of you too, such as what affects your emotions, your mental state, and your spiritual connectedness, not just what affects your physical self. Experimenting with food is worth the effort in helping you to connect with your body so that you can truly have integrated health. Taking care of the earth that is your body so that it can take care of you.

## Awareness Exercise

How your body feels is a direct link to how you feel. If your body isn't feeling well, you tend to not feel well either. But when your body is in its best shape, supported by the best foods for it, and allowed the activity, water, and sleep that it needs, that's when the relationship comes alive with mutual support.

Here is a list of ideas to explore, all centered around your power to take better care of your body. If you like, pick one or two that interest you. This is not medical advice, a diagnosis, or a treatment. Always consult your physician before making any health or medical changes.

- Start a food journal and keep track of what you are eating and how you are feeling. See if there are any patterns.
- Consider a food-elimination program to help you dig up even more information about your body's functioning. There are a lot of programs out there for this so consider your options.
- Schedule your annual physical to check-in on your body.
- See a registered dietician, nutritionist, or functional medicine doctor.
- Choose a book to read on a relevant health topic for you.
- Watch a documentary on health and wellness.
- Do a search for healthy recipes and try something new.
- Increase your water intake and notice how that makes you feel.
- Increase your amount of sleep & notice how that makes you feel.
- Explore what types of physical activity you like.
- Schedule a chat with a personal trainer to see what they offer.
- Look into group fitness opportunities in your area that appeal to you.
- Sing and dance more and notice how that makes you feel.

Give yourself the chance to figure out what works well for you. Through being in partnership with your body, you get to design the personal habits that your body needs to thrive.

## Your Earth-Body Expresses Your Spirit

About a month after my mom passed away in 2001, I got invited to stay with my friend Janie in Joliet, Illinois. She had scored us tickets to go to a bar in Chicago to see a Jerry Cantrell show. Getting away for the weekend was a welcomed invitation, I was excited to see my friend, and I knew Jerry would put on a good show. We arrived at the venue just before the show's start. We waited in line at the bar and each got a bottle of beer. Then we walked through the tight crowd and found a spot center to the stage with people surrounding us on all sides. The room went dark and the stage lights shined a purplish-pink hue on stage as Jerry Cantrell and his band began to perform. I was standing, beer in hand, bopping my head up and down to the music, when I started to feel a rush of warmth come over me. My breath slowed down, and I felt a little woozy. I took another sip of my beer to refresh myself, but the warmth in my face and chest was now feeling strangely fuzzy. I grabbed Janie's arm and said, "I need to go to the bathroom." And then I passed out. Right there on the floor in the middle of the crowded room as Jerry sang on.

The next thing I remember, I was outside the venue and two of the concert staff had me propped up and sitting on the hard concrete sidewalk.

"Are you okay?" Janie was asking as I groggily came to.

One of the staff handed me a water and asked, "Are you on anything?"

I replied, "No, I haven't even had a whole beer yet."

They asked my name, where I was from, and what day it was. I passed all of their tests and was able to stand up. Janie stood with me as I took in more fresh air and decided I felt well enough to go back in. For the rest of the night, I was just fine. We even stopped off at another place to have one more drink before ending the night. I didn't think anything more of it—it seemed to have just been a bizarre and random occurrence.

But then I started to have more random occurrences of feeling that strange, fuzzy warmth and feeling faint, like I was going to pass out. I would get very nervous when this feeling came over me, like I couldn't control it. Sometimes these spells would come on while I was driving, which was really scary. I ended up going to the doctor who told me that I was having panic attacks. *That's weird,* I thought. I didn't feel I was under any stress, not enough to be causing panic attacks, anyway. The doctor ran some labs and found that my thyroid was also not functioning properly and referred me to an endocrinologist who diagnosed me with hypothyroidism.

All summer long, I continued to have bouts of fuzzy panic and was put on medication to balance my thyroid. Then at the end of summer, I went back to Eau Claire to continue with college. About a month in, I got the sickest I had ever been. I threw up for days and felt so weak I couldn't even go to class. Finally, Corey brought me into the emergency room. I was so weak that he had to wheel me in a wheelchair while I sat slumped forward with a barf bucket sitting in my lap. That doctor told me I had a kidney infection. *That's weird,* I thought. I hadn't had a bladder infection recently. I wondered how it was that I ended up with a kidney infection.

In time, the kidney healed, the thyroid issue corrected itself, and the panic attacks stopped. It wasn't until years later, in 2015, when I was taking the AcuEnergetics® Level Three training course with Kevin Niv Farrow that I learned about the kidney energy system and figured out that the string of seemingly random physical ailments that followed the death of my mom were all connected.

I learned that when there is an impeded flow of energy, for both the heart and the kidney's meridian system, anxiety and panic attacks can show up. I also learned that the kidney's energy system governs glands in the body. I then put the pieces together that the thyroid is a gland governed by the kidney's energy. That meant that *all three* of my ailments—panic attacks, thyroid issues, and kidney infection—had been kidney related. Additionally, I learned that the energetic flow of the kidney meridian system can be blocked by the emotion of fear, as in life and death fear, like the fear of losing my mom, and the aftermath of that loss. Suffering this loss had an unsuspected effect on my body. Both mentally and emotionally, I felt like I had done quite well in dealing with Mom's death, but my body knew differently. My body, being connected to my spirit, knew I had experienced a severely severing blow. And what hadn't gotten released through emotional or mental energy, trickled down through my energy field, and its chaos and disorientation settled into my physicality, resulting in illness.

I had already been familiar with how the mind and emotions can cause illness in the body with stress. But I did not know that there are specific connections that link our energetic organ systems to emotions and then to ailment. All humans have the same mapping too—the same meridian and organ systems and the same energy centers that connect to integrate mind, emotion, and spirit with the body.

You too can have energy flows that close down when something happens in your life, like a trauma. It might be that some parts of you seem to be dealing with circumstances around you, but perhaps other parts have shifted into autopilot and are numbing or stuffing away the true depth of your pain. However, your spirit is not fooled. Your holistic self has to have an outlet for that energy to move or it gets stuck, which can cause issues with not only your body but your mind and your emotional stability. The law of energy states that it can neither be created nor destroyed, only transferred. So, energy has to find a place to flow for its tension to dissipate. In my case, my energy of feeling fear bypassed being heavy on my mind and emotions and went straight to my body, affecting the flow of my kidney energy and its related areas. I know now that it is so much gentler on your whole being to disperse energy from trauma *across all four dimensions*. This means allowing the processing of things emotionally, mentally, spiritually, and physically so that no one area bears the brunt or closes down completely in the face of the intensity.

This life lesson is what has encouraged me to use my tools to keep smoothing out my rough edges following the loss of Corey. I talk about the experience, feel the emotions, process the energy of it, seek spiritual connection, and support my body with rest, food, walking, and meditation. In the beginning, I was very worried that my panic attacks would come back in the wake of this awful, heartbreaking experience, so I put into practice everything I could to support *all* of me. I was mindful to stay self-aware and let the pressure release over and over again to avert the possibility that the intensity would show up too much in the physical realm. And it worked. I did have some minor ailments—joint pain, heartache, and stiffness—but nothing monumental because I allowed the energy charge to dissipate across my whole being.

You too can help yourself to process through things by being mindful to have varying outlets through which you can express pent up tensions emotionally, mentally, physically, and even spiritually. Examples could be going for a jog to release physical tension, allowing yourself to have a good cry to release emotional tension, journaling or talking with a trusted person to get your thoughts out in release, and saying some prayers or reading spiritual text, giving your pain to God in spiritual release. Your wholeness is there for you to not only exist in, but to be supported by, as all facets of you work together as one.

## Heaven and Earth Merge in You

The two differentiating dimensions of heaven and earth appear to be dualities, but in their oneness, they are life itself. Both spirit and earth exist around you and within you. No life is separate from the One spirit that gives life to all, and nothing that exists physically is excluded from the energetic source of creation. Sometimes, in your human smallness, you have a contracted perception that keeps you self-focused. Tunnel vision only allows you to be aware of what affects you personally. However, in looking up from your life to the bigness of the life you are a part of, expansion takes place. There is much that you are interconnected with—both on earth and in heaven.

One echo of this is literally and symbolically expressed through the breath of earth. Just like there is really only one ocean, there is really only one breath. One breath that inspirates us all as we all breathe the same air that earth circulates. Imagine the people who have breathed this breath before you and the people who will breathe it in the future. We are all hooked into the same ever-flowing breath of life. Think of the people who are breathing this breath with you now, living life at the same time as you. We are connected in our breath, and that breath is spirit.

And the Lord God formed man of the dust of the ground,

and breathed into his nostrils the breath of life;

and man became a living soul.

–Genesis 2:7

## Connection Practices

Feeling the breath is so much more than physically breathing. Feeling your breath is a way to feel your connection to your source of life, heaven *and* earth, because *in you*, in all of us, is where the two sources meet.

1. Feeling your breath meditation. A reason why sitting and feeling your breath can move you into this sense of connected oneness is that it can help you feel through the layers of the physical into the layers of the spirit. For us here, alive and living on earth, we must use the physical to access heaven. There is no other way. One way through the body to bring more peace and lightness into your life is by engaging in the practice of feeling your breath. In doing so, not only do you open yourself to experience greater peace but you start to become the space for it to move through into the world. Dedicate whatever amount of time a day, even just ten minutes, to practice this meditation so that spirit's extension to the body—the breath—can give back to you.

If every eight-year-old in the world is taught meditation,

we will eliminate violence from the world within one generation.

–Dalai Lama

2. Saying *I love you*'s to the world. Connect to earth around you with your hands by doing the heart-expanding practice I refer to as *saying* your I love you's *to the world.* Your hands are extensions of your heart; they foster connection when you use them with love. Take five minutes to follow these steps:

○ Move freely about your space.

○ As you walk, place your hands on things and say "I love you" to them.

○ Feel your heart as you say this, making a personal connection with an impersonal object.

○ Afterwards, ask yourself: *What did I observe about myself in giving my energy of love freely? How did it feel to do this practice?*

3. Appreciation through gratitude. Take some time to write down or mentally list what on earth you are grateful for and feel the energy of gratitude as you do this. Gratitude fosters the expression of internal connection.

4. Care for the earth in your home or outside by engaging in the upkeep of these spaces. Care fosters expression of external connection. Have you ever noticed that when you clean or pick up clutter the space feels better? There is an energy exchange that takes place. In putting forth your energy to care for your space, it frees up stagnant energy in the space to flow. Also, the order that is created has a positive, tangible feel. Tidy a space and feel how it is different after.

5. Connect with the nature that is your body. If your body is telling you something is wrong, something physical, mental, emotional, or spiritual, it wants you to listen. It could be something you need others' support with, maybe even professional support. Don't ignore your body. What is one day spent at the doctor or a therapist's office in comparison to the rest of your life? Take the time now to invest in yourself.

6. Give yourself nature breaks. Take time to sit in nature and just look at her. Appreciate beauty, notice intricacies, see smallness and

bigness—look for duality in the full expression of nature. Feel yourself in her. Soak in the feeling of being with her in relationship, in connection. And notice how she gives back to you. By spending time in nature surrounded by its glorious beauty, you let your heart be touched and opened.

In everything of earthly and cosmic beauty, you can see a glimpse of something undeniably amazing. It reflects something within yourself that is of cosmic origin—yet it is much harder for you to see your own earthly beauty. But it is there. It is as steady and present as the stars and the moon, even on the dark nights where none shine through. They are there. And so too is your cosmic beauty, even in your own dark nights of life. It is there, within you.

To see a World in a Grain of Sand,

And Heaven in a Wild Flower,

Hold Infinity in the palm of your hand,

And Eternity in an hour.

—William Blake

# 7

# THE UNIFYING PAIR

## *Heart and Mind*

When I transferred colleges and moved to Wisconsin to be with Corey, Sunday was my day to connect to home. It was in the year 2000, so my family still had a land line back home in Michigan. When I called to check in, both my parents would sit on the line, each with a phone to their ear. Usually, however, it would just be Mom and me talking. Dad would quietly listen in and then say, "Bye," at the end. My mom was my home base; in fact, she was home base for our whole family. We all gravitated to her.

After she died, my mind knew she was gone, but my heart knew I still needed someone to hold onto. I had a good relationship with Dad, but we weren't as close as I had been with Mom. During that time, I began working over in my mind a decision to start going to my dad more with things in my life. In doing so, my heart, easing into the huge loss, was able to not feel so alone because I still had him as a parent. It was both my mind and heart together that opened up to connecting deeper with him. We began talking more often, and I started to have conversations with him that I would have had with Mom, sharing my life more openly.

I remember Corey saying during that time: "Your Mom left such a legacy with all of you and how you are as a family." That was a good perspective for me; we still had each other. And in that space of not having Mom but still having each other, new bonds and new dimensions of my relationship with my Dad and my three siblings, started to strengthen. My mind was active in this bonding, but it was actually the heart leading the way in search of what it needed in Mom's absence: connection.

## Evolution Is Changing Relationship

Relationships are ever evolving, just like you are. You don't stay the same in your relationships and your relationships don't stay the same. They either age and mature along with you in deeper connection, or they age and deteriorate in greater disconnect. Sometimes growth in you causes your relationships to change. Sometimes a relationship change affects you. Whether comfortable or uncomfortable, these changes result in a *potential* for connection. With this potential, it is up to you to be intentional, open, and aware about which direction you are moving in your personal evolution.

Disconnect → Dissolution → Separateness

or

Connection → Integration → Unity

The four areas of relationship that you have—with self, others, God, and earth—are integrated. You do not function in them separately because you function as a whole. Although you might give one area more attention or ignore another, they are all important. When a person is low-functioning in one of the four relationships, it does not mean that that relationship doesn't exist; it means they are not connected within it. You cannot be fully alive if you exclude one. Each one is primary in your existence; human beings cannot exist without God, earth, others (thanks, Mom and Dad), and self. You do not exist if there is no you, and there is no you without all four of these relationships.

Each of these relationships makes up a part of your wholeness and how you function. But more than just your existence in them, it is your *depth of connection* with each that supports you in living your life fully integrated as the whole being that you are. You need all areas to be realized with the awareness of your mind and felt with the openness of your heart in order to experience the full richness of the life that is divinely orchestrated for you—with all its complexity and its unity. Your self-awareness is the light of the mind, the light of your consciousness. Openness is the light of the heart. The two combine to make your full capacity to connect and to be connected. These four relationships—with self, others, God, and earth—make up the garden of life in which you grow and evolve. In this garden, the evolution of relationship causes evolution of self.

## Interconnection Can Lend Strength to Weakness

Because of their interconnection, the state of one relationship can bleed into another. A person may feel disconnected from themselves, which causes them to also be disconnected from God, resulting in a sense of separateness. Or, if someone feels disconnected from the earth, they might also feel disconnected from God in God's unity with the earth. Or maybe somebody feels connected to the earth, which then helps them connect with others, promoting a sense of unity. Perhaps in feeling connected to others, somebody has a greater sense of belonging, adding positively to their sense of self and fostering inner connection. Any one relationship that is strong is going to strengthen your potential for connection in the other dimensions. When you have one good relationship, other good relationships can take root. Another example is how the umbrella of faith and trust in God can extend coverage to your relationship with yourself—having faith in yourself that you are on the right path. Also, it can extend to having faith in others and faith in the earth that your needs will be met. This relationship with God, established in faith and trust, doesn't make everything easy, but it allows you to connect with goodness, regardless of challenge, struggle, or strife. Good friendships are like this, too, lending you support no matter the circumstance so you may be stabilized amidst any storm.

Sweet friendships refresh the soul.

–Proverbs 27:9

## The Interconnection of Heart and Mind

When you have poor relationships, it can dim the vibrancy of your other relationships, and the effect becomes somewhat uniform. This dynamic is like a dial where you set your temperature to hot or cold, only this dial sets you to being more open or closed. For example, if you are wounded in one area of life, this can translate into being guarded in other areas. If you are in a contracted holding pattern with some relationships in your life, you need other positive, nourishing relationships to shine light on your being and encourage you to be more open. With supportive relationships, you can turn your dial of openness up, which has an effect across your whole being. But this is not done without personal effort.

Only through honesty with yourself can you have the eyes to see and be intentional in how you are living. Again, openness and awareness are of the heart and the mind together, making up your capacity for connection. The state of your heart is your condition, either open or closed; your mind is the regulator, regulating what the state of your heart's impact is on you. It ends up that the state of your heart colors how your mind perceives, which translates into how you feel and think, which then affects action, or inaction, in your life.

Your level of openness hinges on how self-aware you are about where and how you are. It doesn't necessarily mean you think everything is *just fine* and that you are *open to anything*. That can actually be delusional—a sign of disconnect. You must still use your discernment and navigate life's ups and downs. Openness means you don't turn away. It means you bravely process through and come out better than before: more stable, connected, and vibrantly alive.

While in my studies with Kevin Niv Farrow and AcuEnergetics®, I learned so much about the capacity of the heart. One of Kevin's teachings is that, "The feeling sense is governed by the heart." His insight lends itself to seeing how the duality between heart and mind is that the heart governs your feelings, while the mind governs your thoughts. The nature of mind has a tendency to be contractive as you try to put things in a box by analyzing and explaining. What constricts mind is attachment, such as when you attach to specific thoughts, information, opinions, and perspectives. These can be focal and narrowing. On the other hand, the heart and feeling are expansive. When you allow yourself to feel, you are opening to experience. Whether the feelings are good or bad it doesn't matter; you are inviting self-opening either way.

Another dichotomy is that your heart can feel one way and your mind can think in another. When the two are *not* unified, it is easy to get confused by life. Sometimes there is a separation between thinking about something and feeling it. Maybe it is easier to think about something without the emotion of feeling it. But which do you think is the more connected way of being: thinking about your life or *feeling* your life? The heart is the true connector to your wholeness. Separation between heart and mind breeds inner and outer disconnect. We are separate from ourselves when we live in two different worlds within ourselves: the world of mind and the world of heart. But in their unity, there is connection; you can think about how you feel and have feelings about how you think. When heart and mind come into connective coherence, a synergy emerges *through you* that is both the breathing and beating rhythm of your wholeness.

The longest journey you will make in your life

is from your head to your heart.

−Sioux saying

In my current grief journey, this has been the life-blood of my survival: to have awareness of where I am and to feel where I am, mentally, emotionally, physically, and spiritually. The light of mind and heart working together allows wisdom to shine through and bring clarity and insight, even in the hardest of moments. There have been so many times where the intensity of my pain has been dialed up. Instead of going numb to it, like I had a habit of in earlier years, I have learned to be open to its rawness. I notice that when I let myself feel, the intensity is dialed down a notch as it moves through me.

There have also been times when I observe my thoughts and actions and notice that I am indeed closing down. In the awareness of closing down, I ramp up letting myself feel. I find a person or outlet to express how I am feeling and let it all flow, the heart and the mind.

One example of this was when I was having a hard time during a parent meeting at my kids' school. I was not in a good place that day and could feel my emotions were backing up inside of me, ready to spill over as tears. Tears of sadness that Corey couldn't be there with me like all of the other coupled parents. Tears of sadness that Corey couldn't be there for Marin or for Gavin, to be a part of all of the amazing things they were doing in his absence. I was trying to keep it together and feeling flat and unresponsive to what was actually going on around me in the meeting. I am certain I looked standoffish on the outside, but on the inside I was suffering and trying to hold myself steady as best I could, even if it meant I was a bit frozen and cold. As I stood there among the other parents, I wanted to just run away. Even deeper within me, I wanted to somehow run away from myself.

The next day, I didn't let these feelings and this experience just get swept under the rug. I sought out the opportunity to talk with a friend as I knew I needed to share about the previous day's bottled-up struggle. In the connection of my heart and my mind, I was aware of my need to share openly. Understanding that I have to keep choosing to open to this experience so that life may continue to open to me. By the end of our conversation, we had both shared current struggles and gave loving support. I felt so much better—lighter even—by letting the contents of my mind and my heart come together and flow out from me in expression. But also, better from letting my heart and mind be present with my friend, who was also needing a shoulder of support. Sometimes when life is messy, and we *let it be witnessed as messy*, the messiness becomes cleansing. In connecting with the realness of the mess, the *being real* makes a bigger impact than the mess itself.

In your life as you too see warning glimmers of disconnect show up, it can be tempting to stuff your feelings and turn away from your own thoughts, and emotions, to turn away from your body, or even from the people around you. But when you are in touch with your wholeness, you are gifted a keen eye of wisdom, which can see what is and is not going to be helpful. For instance, when you notice that feeling of the walls closing in on you, you can use a reversal strategy and move to opening instead, by sharing with someone what you are experiencing. In verbally sharing at the same time as you are also open to feeling, the mind and heart will naturally unify and create greater overall coherence in you.

Such awareness and openness gives you an increased ability to move with acceptance through difficulty as the waves of life keep coming. Self-awareness can be your anchoring steadiness in the unsteadiness of life. Connecting you to the experiencing of your life in a more fully balanced way involving head and heart When the heart and mind are not unified, it can show up as letting your mind rule you and being detached from your heart. Or it can show up as letting your emotions rule you and lacking mental stability to take action that is responsive *vs.* reactive. Being too heavily in either the mental or emotional weight of things creates imbalance and perpetuates disconnect. But when the heart and the mind are unified by self-awareness—that stability can open you up to inner wisdom.

## The Combined Wisdom of Heart and Mind

The heart, like the mind, has intelligence, and the mind can also process feelings. They are in a perfect yin-yang relationship, making each other go round to create motion in your life. When the mind's awareness and the heart's openness work together, they are unified. For example, sometimes you need to feel something for yourself to fully understand it. You can be told how to ride a bike, but you can't integrate the instructions until you have a firsthand experience. You have to *feel* how to do it to get it. Or take, for example, faith. You have to feel it to become faithful. You can read and listen and be told about faith, but until your heart opens to feeling faith yourself, you cannot fake experiencing having faith. Faith is a heart-change married to what the mind has absorbed.

In unifying the heart and mind, we are able to function at higher wisdom. This wisdom is really from the light of your soul connecting to your life through your heart. The heart's intelligence has the capacity to integrate and unify with the mind in such a way that the heart's wisdom then goes beyond what your logical mind alone is capable of. This is why advice is often given to *trust your heart*: the heart knows what the mind alone cannot in its connection to your spirit.

The reality of a *bigger-than-mind* capacity of the heart is illustrated through the scientific discovery that the electromagnetic field of the heart is actually sixty times larger than that of the brain. There is a larger capacity for the heart's function than for the brain's. The heart is the real access point for unity, not the mind. You can *think* you are part of a unified One, but until you feel oneness with your heart, you haven't integrated the depth of oneness.

The mind is in better alignment with your soul when it takes its lead from the heart, and when the heart is stable and not in the throes of emotion. You need stability to have an open heart. When the heart is open, the mind is better able to open. Yes, connection is perceived through the mind, but it can only be fostered through the heart. This is yet another example of how you can't think your way into it, you have to feel it. Feeling connection is how you know your connection is real. You arrive at connection through feeling. The heart is the great connector. The heart is the relational root. Because of this, the heart is *how* you navigate relationship. The heart forgives, the heart has compassion, the heart is capable of acceptance. You can't just think these things into being; you have to feel them for it be genuine.

When openness and awareness, and your mind and heart, work cohesively, and wisdom is able to blossom, you brush up against your capacity for acceptance. You can feel a bit freer from personal suffering when you have acceptance in your heart. You are no longer striving for perfection; you are simply living as a human being with strengths and weaknesses. And you are able to see others in the same light of acceptance. This brings you to the space from which your heart is meant to be functioning for your own good, for the good of others, for the good of the earth, and for the good of God.

The Lord does not look at the things people look at.

People look at the outward appearance, but the Lord looks at the heart.

−1 Samuel 16:7

## Separated by Language; Connected by Acceptance

When I think of acceptance, the story of the Tower of Babel comes to mind. It is a story from the book of Genesis, which is both Jewish and Christian.

> Now the whole world had one language and a common speech. As people moved eastward, they found a plain in Shinar and settled there.
>
> They said to each other, "Come, let's make bricks and bake them thoroughly." They used brick instead of stone, and tar for mortar. Then they said, "Come, let us build ourselves a city, with a tower that reaches to the heavens, so that we may make a name for ourselves; otherwise we will be scattered over the face of the whole earth.
>
> But the Lord came down to see the city and the tower the people were building. The Lord said, "If as one people speaking the same language they have begun to do this, then nothing they plan to do will be impossible for them. Come, let us go down and confuse their language so they will not understand each other.
>
> So the Lord scattered them from there over all the earth, and they stopped building the city. That is why it was called Babel— because there the Lord confused the language of the whole world. From there the Lord scattered them over the face of the whole earth. (Genesis 11:1–9)

When I first read this creation story, I thought, *I don't get it. Why would God want to do that?* I wondered: *wouldn't God want us to come together, not divide us further? What would be the purpose of this?* Then I began to ponder the story in relation to acceptance, and it started to come together for me. That which was made different in us, in this story our differing languages, was actually made to connect us, not separate us. In having our differences made apparent, it first appears that our ability to connect and work together is taken from us, but instead it is only setting the stage for *God's work in us* to be amplified. Because the way in which we are able to connect and work together through any difference is by way of the heart. It is as if God is saying in this story: *If your heart is separate from me—I must give you a way for your heart to come back to me by getting you to use your heart, not your hands, for great acts.* In this story it is shown that the divide from God *in action* was due to being divided from him in heart. When the heart can see beyond differences in acceptance, that is not an act of the human hand, but an act of the human heart, which is *God's* masterpiece that *He built* in us. Perhaps it ends up being that the purpose in difference and duality, and all that appears to divide us, is to bring us back to oneness with God and with each other. In seeing the differences among us and making it less about reaching a personal-great and more about seeing a united-great, we build what God truly intended us to build: that love-thy-neighbor-greatness that is built through connection and open-hearted acceptance.

Teacher, which is the greatest commandment in the Law?

Jesus replied: "Love the Lord your God with all your heart

and with all your soul and with all your mind."

This is the first and greatest commandment.

And the second is like it: "Love your neighbor as yourself."

–Matthew 22:36–40

Can it get any simpler than this? Why do we humans complicate things so much? I think it's because the human mind is not yet attached to the heart well enough, and the human heart is not yet in working order. With acceptance, there is a coming together *through* that which was pulling apart. A coming together *through* the differences, *because of* the differences. A connection made through that which was causing the disconnection. Perhaps there is a little bit of wisdom in this story to help you understand this idea of differences created through God—and for what purpose? We must overcome what is different on the surface and be united through what is deeper. And that depth is not skin-deep, it is heart-deep. God created us differently on the outside and the same on the inside. When you look deeper, you are able to see we are all the same. The difference in human language is surface, but understanding is deep. People are still able to understand one another despite their language differences. The pain people feel is the same. Sadness is sadness. Anger, worry, joy, peace, and love are universal. And that is the language of the heart, which is deeper than the language of the tongue. The constructs of man separate us, but the constructs of God—the heart—unify us.

## The Toxin Can Become the Medicine

It is our spiritual work, our human work, and our earthly work to take root in the heart of connection, to grow the eyes to see deeper, and to reach this place of depth within duality— *because of* duality. The thing that pulls us apart can bring us together; the thing that divides, unifies. This story of Babel speaks to God's effort not to disconnect us from God but to bring us to Him. God needs us to see *how* we are divided in heart. In the end, it's not really our differences that divide us, it's our attachment to our differences. We can easily be united in our differences by seeing where we relate. Are we not all human?

This possibility lies in how the toxin can also be the medicine. A small part of that which is toxic can be given to heal. The same thing that starts in you as a poisonous taste for intolerance—such as orienting towards difference in language, creed, nation, or opinion—is in God's sovereign way designed to be the medicine through which acceptance can be grown. Is there someone you are intolerant of who seems different than you? Who comes to mind? Perhaps they are in your life to do just the opposite: to create a space for tolerance *vs.* to drive a wedge between you and them.

One who was once toxic in judgment can become supportive in acceptance when the wisdom of connection takes shape in heart and mind. Any two that appear to be pitted against each other are also designed to play a part in coming together for the healing of humanity. Your differences are designed to lead you back to the heart in acceptance, seeing we are all just human. By coming together in our differences, we reach the space of unity, where the toxin becomes an integrated part of the medicine.

Using a toxin to treat the illness is echoed in our physical medicines, like homeopathy and immunizations. In homeopathy, they *treat like with like.* When someone comes in for homeopathic treatment, they look at the person's symptoms and treat the person with remedies that would normally make a person sick with the same symptoms that the person is already suffering from. The effect of using that which would be a toxin for a healthy person is that the toxin acts as a medicine for the ill. In regard to immunization, science has shown that giving the toxic substance in a small dose—like for chickenpox, measles, and polio—actually acts as a medicine, preventing the individual from falling deeply ill from the toxin itself. Where a little bit of a toxin stimulates the cure, it is not accidental, it is by design.

## Opening to Life Opens You to Flow

Acceptance is having an open and aware connection within duality. Accepting you are going to have goodness in your life and you are going to have bad, too. Accepting you are going to have triumphs and struggles because living in fullness is what makes you whole. Unity in duality. Acceptance of duality is unifying because it allows you to be *in flow* with the cycles and rhythms of life. The duality of the good and the bad still exists, but they are intimately connected and integrated. There is no interruption where one ends and the other begins; there is just the flow of life—like the river, like the breath. You need to accept both the inhales and exhales, the contractions and expansions, of life. Breathing is being in flow. When you hold your breath against things, in avoidance or deception, flow is impeded. Restricting flow is unnatural. Flow is natural. Don't be afraid to breathe your life, to live your life, to be open to your life.

In the first several weeks after Corey's death, everything in me wanted to bind up and freeze. However, because of my knowledge of the body-mind-spirit-emotion connection, I knew nothing helpful would come of allowing myself to completely shut down. So, with awareness and courage, I let myself feel everything I was feeling. I didn't hide crying in front of our kids. I sobbed uncontrollably during each shower, and I felt all of the anger and fear that was trying to take me over. And I breathed. In fact, breathing was one thing that offered me a balancing effect during this important, heavy processing. It supported inner flow by connecting my attention to the movement and essence of the breath. And it helped my feelings to stabilize by giving space between thoughts. I also started walking daily, giving me even more physical and energetic support. I was open to flow from two different angles. First, allowing myself to *be* in the flow of feeling my emotions, not stamping them down or brushing them off. Second, *creating* flow through meditating on the breath and walking. Here again is *being* and *doing*, the complimentary and purposeful pair of being open to both ends of the spectrum of life. And even though it was incredibly difficult, I believe I fared better by being in flow with my process.

## Music as Flow is a Connector for Your Heart

During the first six months of processing my grief, I had many moments where the flow of mind, body, heart, and spirit were all able to converge in a therapeutic way. And the connecting catalyst that brought me there was music. From April through October, until it started to get too cold, I would go outside by myself, walk laps around our yard, and listen to music. As I moved my body, the music moved me.

Having this routine began by listening to the playlists that we had exchanged on our last Valentine's Day together, two months before Corey passed. The exchange was just something simple and sweet I had suggested we do, since we never usually made a big deal about the holiday. I remember getting his list of songs in my phone on Valentine's Day and scrolling through them, smiling at the *us* songs that he had picked: "Springsteen," by Eric Church, "Room at the Top," by Tom Petty, "Windfall," by Son Volt, and "Run," by George Strait, to name a few. I still can vividly picture him sitting in his chair in the living room, listening through snippets of the songs on the playlist I created for him. There was one song he stopped at and thoughtfully listened to: "Right Down the Line," by Gerry Rafferty.

"When I wanted you to share my life,

I had no doubt in my mind.

And it's been you, woman,

Right down the line."

As he finished listening to the song, he looked up at me with a smile on his face and said, "I love it." This is just one of the reasons why those playlists we exchanged and the music they contain mean so very much to me. They contain our life. In those songs were woven memories from our lives together —funny moments, tender moments, and also thoughts and feelings we held for each other. The preciousness of it all easily brought tears as I walked, feeling movement in my grief.

As time went on, I started to create a new playlist for myself. The songs I compiled over the months captured how I was feeling. They resonated with my own inner voice but also enabled me to hear his voice, in a way. To still hear *our* voice. Some songs felt like they were another *us* song, or an *us now* song, like "Starting Over," by Chris Stapleton.

"It don't matter to me,

Wherever we are's where I wanna be.

And honey, for once in our lives,

Let's take our chances and roll the dice.

I can be your lucky penny.

You can be my four-leaf clover,

Startin' over."

The words in these new songs spoke of how I missed Corey, how I loved him, how deep our love truly was and still is. They also spoke to the hope of what might be left for me in life, ongoing. In fact, this music contained just as much hope as it did sadness—both of which needed to be felt. And by feeling both my ups and my downs in wholeness, with all dimensions of my being integrated into these heart-reaching musical walks, a strange and amazing thing started to happen: my sadness became comforting. I began to have moments where it actually felt good to connect in with my sadness, because along with the sadness, I could feel the sweetness of love. I could feel that the sadness was there so deeply, because so too was the love. My sadness was refracted through the prism of love in me, bending it in such a way that, instead of it just appearing as sadness, I could see a fuller spectrum of emotion shining through, like a rainbow. I was feeling the full color-range of human emotion—from sadness to love. I was feeling it all, in wholeness.

Music was a connective force for Corey and I since the very beginning. I believe that it is likely to be a force for you, too. You can feel connection through music *because* music has the gift of being able to speak your life to you. Music is a gift of flow: a pure expression of life in all of the sounds, feelings, and words that color it. Music is expression and experience. Music is transcendental connection, breaking through all dimensions to the whole of our humanness. Someone creating music has inspiration that moves through their spirit to create, and often there is an emotional tie to their creation as well. It takes mental energy to create lyrics, harmony, and melody and then fit it all together in a flow of physical instruments and voice. And then music is physically, emotionally, mentally, and spiritually experienced. You take in the beats and the words with your body and your mind. But then the music goes deeper, touching your emotion and your spirit.

Music is the universal language of the world. Everybody naturally connects to it. The type you connect with might be different than the next person, just like there are different languages in the world, but for all of us, music is an amplification of what is in our hearts. At times, the language of music speaks to you individually about where you are at and what you're going through. Self-awareness is enlightened in it—expressing something you haven't been able to put into words. And sometimes, God communicates to your heart through it.

## A Practice to Create Heart Flow

As life brings you to moments that invite your heart to open, keep in mind that anything that is heart-opening is healthy for your body, mind, emotions, and spirit. Anything that is heart-opening is good for the relationships that you have with yourself, others, God, and the earth. You can experience heart change from the outside in by letting external circumstances shape your heart's openness. But you can also be more direct by inciting a heart change from the inside out through personal practices that open the heart to more flow. In opening your heart flow, the emotional, mental, physical, and spiritual energy of your heart is allowed freedom to move instead of being held in contraction. When the heart has more flow, you feel more connected and in sync with life. You can have greater resilience, acceptance, and joy, as well.

My favorite practice for opening the flow of the heart is a meditation called *the inner smile*. This practice done consistently over time has the potential to change you from the inside out, bringing heart and mind into cohesion, your heart more inclined to openness, and your mind more aware. The inner smile is an ancient practice, but I was taught it by Kevin Niv Farrow in my studies of AcuEnergetics®. Meditation is a medicine in its own right. Its effects branch across mind, body, emotion, and spirit. This is why so much research shows the holistic effects of practicing meditation, from decreasing physical tensions, like the compounds of stress, and even lowering blood pressure. There are studies that show it improves concentration and mental focus and that it supports emotional stability and resilience. The reach of the practice of meditation is multidimensional because the practice itself is holistic. And this one specifically aims at relaxing the heart and opening up through the feeling of love.

- Get comfortable, close your eyes, and take a moment to feel your breath.

- Next, think of something that makes you smile. It can be anything: a memory, a person, or the thought of baby giggles or puppy snuggles.

- Once you are smiling, drop the thought and shift your awareness from your mind into your heart-center and feel in the center of your chest, noticing simply how you feel.

- When the mind wanders, come back to a thought that triggers your smile and, when you are smiling again, shift into your feeling sense and be aware at your heart center.

- Keep moving through these same motions over and over, with naturalness and ease.

- In regard to how much time to spend doing this practice, fifteen minutes is a great start and daily is the most beneficial. You can use a timer to signal when your time is done.

- Additionally, if you prefer a guided meditation, I have recorded one for you that is fifteen minutes in length at the following link: www.korinn.com/resources.html

Be open in your practice; no need to make it a job or a struggle. Simply open your heart to experiencing you, however you might be, feeling yourself in the simplicity of the inner smile. In doing this practice, you are never *trying* to change your heart. The opening potential of this simple practice is what allows your heart to open on its own. As heart flow increases, you will feel the benefit—perhaps as a mental or emotional change, or maybe a softening of thoughts or edges. It could even show up as a physical change, like feeling more relaxed in your body. Heart work is good work, deserving of your time and attention.

A cheerful heart is good medicine, but a crushed spirit dries up the bones.

—Proverbs 17:22

Above all else, guard your heart, for everything you do flows from it.

—Proverbs 4:23

# 8

# THIS IS NOT THE END

## *This is Your Beginning*

I felt a twinge of anger mixed with disgust as I spied a couple walking hand-in-hand on the pier. Gavin rode ahead of me on his bike. Marin was beside me on her scooter. We had come downtown to enjoy the sunny July day and take our minds off the funeral that would be happening soon. I had a little space to let myself be in my head, so I brought my awareness to this feeling of hate that was spreading inside of me. My stomach tightened and my throat center closed down.

I felt like I wanted to say to the couple, "Screw you."

Of course, I knew I would never do that, but I was thinking it. The sad anger inside of me was reacting to Corey not being here to walk with us or to hold my hand ever again. It burned me from the inside-out as I watched the couple smile at each other and the lady lean in a little closer to her man. My flames of emotion found the couple to be a fitting target for my pain to flare towards, as I shot eye-daggers at the unsuspecting pair. I knew this was irrational—being mad at two strangers because I could not be with my love anymore; and yet, it was exactly how I was feeling, so I let myself feel it.

As I kept walking, I changed my view to see where Gavin was. I spotted him ahead. He had turned around and was coasting on his bike back towards us, smiling. As I looked into his big brown eyes, I could feel all of those binding sensations leave my body. He was not a trigger for my pain, he was a help to it. I looked at Marin, who was just a little behind me. She looked so content, so in the moment, so free. The peaceful look on her face made me smile. I felt blessed by God to have them. Then I looked out across the water at the handful of sailboats anchored in the little bay. It was a beautiful sight that caused me to pause to capture this moment, for my heart's sake. I thought about how, only moments before, I had been disturbed, but how easy it was to shift my focus back to the goodness in my life. It was a beautiful day, even though our family four-pack was minus one. I knew that the sadness of missing Corey would always be there. I would never stop carrying it, because it was a part of me and my life now, but so was the life I had left to live. So, I let the rest of the walk take me to a place where my heart could feel fuller through connecting with the gratitude, joy, and lightheartedness that was still possible for me.

My heart still ices over at times, but I won't let it completely freeze. In between the times when my grief and my life get the best of me, I am sure to warm my heart so that the iciness can thaw. I am careful to not let it grow any thicker and harden in permanence. I am making sure to stay connected to my heart, as it is my connection to everything else. I watch it, I feel it, I let it be felt, and then I consciously give it space to open in its pain, and to its love. I keep doing this over and over. It has become my practice: feel the sadness, feel the pain, feel the warmth, repeat. Although, I notice the practice has become less of something I have to think about and more of just the way that I am. By being aware and open with my heart and mind, I am in the flow of my process—not blocking life, but opened to living.

My personal goal is to reach a point where the warmth of my heart becomes the norm again, and the pain is sprinkled in, in smaller amounts, so that I am not drowning in it anymore. I trust the pain will dull in time, but that the wound will never fully go away. Neither will the love. I am discovering it is possible that you can have both pain and love in your heart but that, in the midst of both, you can only be one way: open or closed. Open to feeling the pain and the love, or closed off from the pain and the love. When you are open, you are connected. When you are closed, you are disconnected. In connection, the pain softens in the light of love. And in disconnection, your love is shrouded in the sharpness of the pain. Pain is so much easier to weather when the warming rays of love keep breaking through the dark clouds. Thank God for all that is a warming ray of love in your life.

## Life Is Continuous

Despite the ups and downs of life, there is continuity. You keep going. You keep going when it is hard. You keep going when it is easy. Beginnings and endings happen all the time. Things change in your life, like the seasons, like the years, like the body. Among all of the many changes, the new beginnings, and final endings, the continuum that is strung through all of it is that *this is your life*. The endings and beginnings merge into the bigger oneness that is your life's continuum. Even when you take breaks, the flow of life keeps moving you forward. But now you get to decide how you want to be, how you want to continue, in your process.

You are a process at the same time you are a product. The process is what you do to create who you are. Who you are, here and now, is the product that emerges, moment to moment, from the process you are in. Empower yourself to use your current process to become a greater product of good. This is done through having relationships of heart-opening connection. The connection you can have in each of the four relationships can give you the goodness you seek. The more connected you are in them, the stronger you are and the fuller life feels. The less connected you are, the weaker you are, and the more fragmented you feel. At any time, if you are feeling a disconnect in any area of your life, you can take inventory to see where you are in all four primary relationships. This will give you a launching point. Whether the disconnect is personal or professional, with an individual or group, an inner or an outer disconnect, with God or with the world at large, you can use the difficulty for good because it is in your *process of reconnecting* that good can come.

## Where Are You Now in the Continuum of Your Life?

With life as your continuum, the things that have happened in your past have led you to where you are today. Likewise, the things that will be happening in your tomorrows have been built up from your past and your today. This is why *letting go* and *moving on* is not so easy—everything becomes a part of you and is carried forward with you. However, sometimes it is up to you to decide what the purpose of your past is. Is its purpose to make you a more closed human being or to make you a more open-hearted human being? You may not know you have a say in this, but you do. You can direct yourself towards how you want to be.

Perhaps it is a better approach to not compartmentalize pieces of your life, packing life into little boxes you can make look pretty on the outside … or tuck away in a dark corner of an inner closet. Give your life air. You are not a closet to hide things away in; you are a beautiful tapestry, a true work of art. You are the display of the story of your life—a story that is still being written. Some things, like hard times and emotions, are going to be there because you are human, but you get to add to your story. So, what do you want to include? What picture do you want to create with the tapestry of your life? It's okay to have anger and sadness weaved in along with the love, but let the love rule and guide you. Let the love draw you to the colorful feelings you want to add and let it guide your heart as you work at building upon what is a part of your life today. Accept the things you cannot change and move with them in a healthy way. The things that have caused you to feel disconnected have less power to do so when you are connected to your wholeness.

Taking personal inventory can illuminate your area of disconnect within the four relationships. It can be an indicator of where you are weak and need to invest time and attention to produce greater integrated support for the challenges in your life. Taking inventory can also give insight into where you are strong so that you can lean into these supportive relationships as you navigate difficulty. In both directions, from weakness or from strength, invest in goodness to launch yourself. The goodness you invest in your relationships will not be one-sided. As you open your heart to give, you likewise open your heart to receive. Regardless of what area in life your difficulty is, connection will be like opening an umbrella on a rainy day, giving you more coverage by opening to fullness.

## Create a Connection Plan to Support Where You Are

It is now time to gather perspective so that you can develop a personalized, four-week plan for the purpose of supporting yourself at this time. First, connect with yourself by answering the following open-ended questions. You can record this in your journal:

1.  *What is my difficulty in life right now?*
2.  *How do I feel disconnected in this difficulty?*
3.  *What result would I like to produce for myself?*

By being open and honest with yourself, you can move further into perspective and clarity about where you are in each of the four relationships. The four relationships are going to be your support in getting the positive result you want. This is because these connections support heart-opening, and an open heart is like a skeleton key: it can unlock any door you have closed within yourself.

*Draw this diagram in your journal.*
*Then write a percent on the line indicating*
*how connected you feel to each aspect of life.*

Self    0%————————— 50% —————————100%

Others  0%————————— 50% —————————100%

God    0%————————— 50% —————————100%

Earth  0%————————— 50% —————————100%

This is the same self-inventory you took in Chapter One, so it might be insightful to go back to your ratings from when you began the journey of this book to see if any changes are already starting in you. In regards to today's fresh assessment, look at where you are in connection to each of the four relationships. Which relationship should you work on? It might make sense to choose the area that is weakest to begin with, but also feel free to use your intuition to make your selection. Write this relationship down in your journal and know that, no matter what your selection is, the end-result will be a plan of action that you can move towards, bringing heart-opening connection into your life. You are also welcome to come back later and work on another relationship, creating another plan of action as well.

Your plan of action will become your process. Plan to give attention to working within your selected relationship for the purpose of strengthening it and the whole of your life. To create your action items, you will write in your journal a list of possible things you can do to connect within your selected relationship. (This might be a good time to think back to some of the tools you have explored in this book, or look back through the chapters for ideas.)

The torch that has been lit is now passed on to you. Take this light of awareness, knowing that it is up to you alone to put into practice your connection plan for the next four weeks. After four committed weeks, take the inventory above again to see if you've had any connective heart changes. Feel into your process to see what you are producing as you build your relationship. Then decide if you need more time with the one you've been working on or if you would like to build connection in a different relationship area. Follow your heart in your process. And keep in mind that you are not looking for perfection but *connection* and awareness in connection. The issue of disconnection is solved by self-awareness and open-heartedness, honesty, time, and effort—not perfection. So, be okay with your process being messy and grow in accepting what is.

To give you an example, I will share my personal plan of action. I rated myself lowest in my relationship with the earth, so I picked that relationship to work on. My personal ideas to practice were:

1. Walk in nature.
2. Give thanks to healthy foods for nourishing me.
3. Charge water energetically by holding a cup of water and saying out loud, "I love you," and then drinking the charged water.
4. Spend five minutes a day looking out the window, doing nothing but watching the natural world.
5. Watch a nature documentary.
6. Ask my body what it needs daily and listen to its reply.

I have created a four-week calendar for you to use to keep on track. It is available at the back of the book or can be printed at: www.korinn.com/resources.html.

## Connection Is Wholeness

In connection, we feel whole and unified. Your heart longs for connection because it longs for unity—with yourself, other human beings, in the larger world, and in the bigger story that is being written in life on earth through God.

When you're going through a tough time, use the four relationships to stabilize you and give you the connective strength and support to get you through. You can be supported in faith and understanding of God—something bigger than yourself. You can be supported by others who identify, validate, witness, and love you. You can be supported in connection with yourself to know which direction to go, what path to take, and when to let yourself rest. And you can be supported in connection and nourishment from the outside world of earth. When you have established connection to them, these four relationships will give back to you in times of need.

Keep in mind that through the four relationships, it is really *one* integrated way of being. Remember the dial? Open or closed? Choosing one relationship to build gives you a touch point to connect with so that you can open in general. And in your heart's openness, you are better able to connect to the universal feeling of love. Love that spreads across all dimensions of beingness. It is a love that unites you to yourself and to all outside of you. It is the medicine that you can make and send out into the world, that will ultimately give back to you.

> Friendship is the only cement that will ever hold the world together.
>
> –Woodrow Wilson

During this very difficult time in my life, connection has been my saving grace. I am grateful for each of the relationships that I have, as they have helped me to keep getting through. I have had self-awareness as support, other people as support, and God as my big champion. I have had good food and healthy activities to support me. I have taken trips to water, a naturally soothing and cleansing source, and have been surrounded by the beauty in nature. I also have had my husband, Corey, whose eternal spirit is able to reach through the ethers of heaven to earth, connecting to the part of me open enough to hear his heart's language. He showed me that love does go on, giving me a sense of knowing that, through each of the four relationships, there is love to go on with.

What is established now carries on in your soul. The love you have with God, yourself, other people, and things of this world won't fade when you pass on someday. Your heart can keep them in full color. I imagine that they hold steady within the heart as an eternal part of you in the great beyond. That might just be the greatest gift of integrated connection: experiencing the truth that love has no boundary and is truly eternal.

In still being connected to the love Corey and I share, I am able to hear his heart-message to me. In one such moment, it came through in a song—a place where we could still be together, even though we are apart. As I listened, I knew. I knew that he was reaching out to me. I knew what he was saying and felt the open-hearted truth in it. The song was "While You Still Can," by the Brothers Osborne. It goes like this:

"'Cause everything you thought would last forever

Never lasts forever, like you plan

Don't let your now become a never

So take life by the hands while you still can."

It's saying: live with an open heart because…you can. And in our connectedness, this message, this song, this truth, is not just for me—it is also for you. This is where my story ends and yours begins. "So, take life by the hands while you still can."

## Closing Letter

While writing this book, I had a prayer that I would read each day when I sat down to write.

Dear God,
You have written a story in me. How can I write a story in you that reflects what you want the world to know?
Love,
Korinn

We all have a story. We all are God's story. His story in you is still being written. Would you like to be more in-tune with what His meaning in your story is?

Music is essentially twelve notes between any octave.

Twelve notes and the octave repeats.

It's the same story told over and over.

All the artist can offer the world is how they see those twelve notes.

—*A Star Is Born* (2018)

We are all just different degrees of the same thing. All you can offer is *how you are* as an artist of light creating life through connection, connection, connection . . . and experience, exploration, understanding, openness, love, gentleness, kindness, and expansion. I hope that this book has encouraged the song playing forth from you in your life. And I pray that your heart keeps opening to all of the beauty it contains so that you too may share the story that is you *alive* in the world.

And finally, a new prayer in completion of this book—one for us to pray together:

Dear God,

Please unite us in our differences so that we may not feel separate because of them.

Love,

All of Us

Amen

*The world is filled with many different eyes to see through*

*But there is only one way our eyes can be opened to seeing—with love.*

## Acknowledgments

My list is small, but my indebtedness big. First, acknowledging the co-creators and inspirations in my life: Corey, Gavin, and Marin. Love you big! Next out, family and close friends: I have learned through you, and with you, as we share life. And to the teachers from whom I have learned a host of goodies that I savor in my soul. To all of the above: you will see yourselves in these pages because I did not arrive here without having the privilege of your story being woven into mine. And I'll wrap up all my love and thanks for each of you in a big bow of thanks to God, the creator, that has positioned us to be here, together. With much appreciation, thank you.

## About the Author

Korinn S. Hawkins is the founder and lead instructor of Moms of Meditation (momsofm.com), which is dedicated to helping mothers deepen their lives through online meditation courses. Korinn has a background as an energy therapist and is trained in AcuEnergetics®. She is also the author and illustrator of several children's books. She lives in western Wisconsin with her family. To learn more about her and her offerings, visit Korinn.com.

If you have enjoyed this book, please support Korinn as an independent author by sharing it with others.

# The Four Relationships
## Connection Plan

Write a percent on the line indicating how connected
you feel right now in each of the following relationships:

Self      0% ----------------------------50%----------------------------100%

Others    0% ----------------------------50%----------------------------100%

God      0% ----------------------------50%----------------------------100%

Earth    0% ----------------------------50%----------------------------100%

o Pick the weakest one, or the one that calls to you, and
  plan to give attention to working within that relationship.
o You may want to read that relationship's chapter again.
o In the following chart, write a list of things you can do to
  strengthen that relationship.
o Put these ideas into practice for four weeks and then
  take the assessment again.

Date_____

(printable at www.korinn.com/resources.html)

# CONNECTION MONTH

| Sunday | Monday | Tuesday | Wednesday | Thursday | Friday | Saturday |
|--------|--------|---------|-----------|----------|--------|----------|
|        |        |         |           |          |        |          |
|        |        |         |           |          |        |          |
|        |        |         |           |          |        |          |
|        |        |         |           |          |        |          |
|        |        |         |           |          |        |          |

## RELATIONSHIP STRENGTHENING PRACTICES

*List and number, then record the number on the calendar for each day you practice that item*